THE TEENAGE RIDER'S HANDBOOK

A Guide for Buying, Training, Showing, Selling

Barbara J. DeWorken
&
Lori Gordon

Sterling House
Pittsburgh, PA

Sterling House Trade Paperback
ISBN 1-56315-046-8

© Copyright 1997 by Babara DeWorken and Lori Gordon
All rights reserved
First Printing—1997

Request for information should be addressed to:

Sterling House Publisher
The Sterling Building
440 Friday Road
Department T-101
Pittsburgh, PA 15209

Printed in the United States of America

TABLE OF CONTENTS

# PREFACE

What special need and what particular audience does this book address, which makes it so different from tons of other horse books on the market, on every subject from breeding to training to showing? The answer is that this book has been designed expressly for the **intermediate to advanced teenage rider (guy or gal) who plans to buy, train, show, and perhaps even sell his own horse, for competition in open shows in Western Pleasure, Hunter Under Saddle, Western Horsemanship, and Hunt Seat Equitation.**

Lori Gordon, a professional horse marketing expert and horse show judge, and Barb DeWorken, a professional educator, writer, and lifelong horseperson, experienced as a riding instructor and horse trainer, provide a step-by-step, question/answer, lesson plan approach, which centers on the principles of perception, patience, planning, and performance. The text reaches into both the mind of the teen rider and his/her horse, to show the rider how both can develop physically and mentally as a performance team.

Chapters focus on the rider's goals and abilities, assessing the abilities and training of a horse before purchase, matching the abilities of horse and rider, maintaining the health and fitness of the show horse and the rider, planning daily training routines from basics to the polished performance, grooming the horse and outfitting the rider for the show ring, planning strategies for the warmup ring and show ring, and applying sound marketing principles for selling the show horse. A special feature of the book is that it can be used as a guide at each step along the way, both at home and away from home.

A LOOK IN THE MIRROR:
Matching the Rider's Goals with his abilities

You have made the big decision. After sitting on the sidelines for show season after show season, watching friends or neighbors compete in the show ring, you have finally decided that it is time for you and your horse to join in the fun and excitement. You are going to show your horse. Great! But what do you do next? How do you prepare yourself and your mount to enter that ring, where all of those friends and neighbors, maybe even your parents, and, most importantly, a judge will have their eyes on your every move? What if you don't even own your own horse yet or can't even afford to buy one? Then, what do you do? Well, you have started in the right place, with this chapter on goals.

As the chapter title says, whether you are a guy or a gal, you must take a close look at yourself and match your goals with your abilities, even before you think about how your horse fits into the picture. Thus, this first chapter looks at you, the rider, and the people around you who may influence you in your decision making. Let's take a look at some important quesions.

WHAT ARE YOUR GOALS AS A COMPETITOR?

Plainly and simply, in what show ring classes do you see yourself realistically competing for the upcoming season? For next year? For two or three years down the road? During your years as a college student or as a young adult who must work for a living after graduating from high school? How do you answer this question? First, attend some horse shows (as you probably already have) and talk to successful competitors about the classes in which they are now showing and in which they began to show.

Talk to the people in the judge's booth, when they have a free moment, and, if possible, talk to the judge him/herself. Be sure to attend the types of shows in which you see yourself competing.

If there is a 4-H group in your area, talk to the leaders and attend some shows. Check tack store and/or feed store bulletin boards, the bulletin board at the barn where you are now riding, and watch the classified ads in the newspaper for upcoming "open" shows sponsored by various clubs or associations.

Once you have some opinions, match them up against this scenario. Usually, you start with the more basic classes, and as you and your horse advance in showing ability, you move to more challenging work. Thus, even if you are able to ride the canter, for example, if you do not feel comfortable doing your first couple of shows at that gait, enter a beginner's class for walk/trot only. Learn the ropes. Get comfortable with the procedures. Get your horse and yourself used to the surroundings. Then, advance to pleasure classes before you go on to more advanced work like jumping, for English riders, or horsemanship, for Western riders. Set up a plan of where you see yourself ultimately competing. This idea brings us to the next question.

WHY ARE YOU SHOWING IN THE FIRST PLACE?

Some young riders, and adults as well, show for the fun of it. To them it is a hobby that allows friendly competition without the pressure or the devotion of time and money required in a more business-like program. If that is your goal, great! You can compete in enough shows each season to build your experience, but you will not have to "push it" to attend rain or shine to gain points for a regional or state championship that will look good on a resume. If you see yourself building a reputation as a serious competitor who will make his living with horses, that's another story. You will need to invest more time, money, and dedication to advance enough to get yourself noticed in the local and maybe even regional or state horse community. You must make these decisions, maybe not this minute, but soon, so that your focus will remain clear.

And what about the idea of winning that coveted blue ribbon? As with any other sport, enough wins will come to him/her who works with persistence and dedication over a period of time. If all you want is lots of blue ribbons, you are forgetting about all those steps in between the beginner and the winner. Whether you show horses for fun or for profit, you will need to take all of those steps to success, one step at a time. If you can't or won't see this truth, you doom yourself and your horse to tons of frustration and tension, to pushing too hard too fast, and to ruining your hopes of what you might have attained.

Okay, so the next problem is all of those friends, neighbors, and even your parents, who have ideas about what your goals should be too. How do you handle them? It is important to make sure your decisions about the abilities and goals of you and your horse are based on sound, expert advice and common sense, not just on emotion or on spur-of-the-moment thinking. (More about expert advice later in this chapter. As you read, you will see that you also need to think through some other things mentioned in this chapter before deciding to seek out an expert.)

No doubt many friends and neighbors will offer you well-intentioned opinions. Before you go off in ten different directions at once, consider the source of the information. If you have friends or neighbors who would rather trail ride for fun than show at all, maybe they will discourage you from showing, because they don't want to lose a riding buddy on the trails. Maybe they are even jealous of you for setting goals higher than theirs. Maybe they would prefer that you have free time to spend with them on non-horsy activities. Maybe, on the other hand, they are excited and happy for you, so happy that they urge you to do too much too fast, because they would love to see your rapid rise to success. Maybe they want you to show in exactly the same kinds of classes they show in, whether you and your horse are ready, willing, and able, or not. You will have to sort out all of these and many other possibilities in your mind, as you consider their opinions about what you plan to do with your time, money, and horse. You still have to face these friends and neighbors, but you have a life and goals too. Do some serious thinking about what's most important to you at this stage in your life and for the next few years to come. Okay, think you've gotten your head on straight? Now, what about your parents?

Let's face it; until you are an independent adult, your parents have a lot to say about how you are developing as a person. Of course, they have that right and they want the best for you, even if your relationship with them doesn't run super smoothly all of the time, or they don't always seem to say what they truly mean. (Think about it. Are you always a perfect communicator?) They could be very negative, very positive, or somewhere in between, depending on a lot of factors. One factor is their own knowledge of horses. Another is their hopes for your future. Another is family responsibilities, including time and money spent on you and your siblings. (More about time, money, and responsibilities as this chapter continues.)

If they are negative, do you fear you will be arguing toe-to-toe with them without any hopes of seeing eye to eye? Do you

have visions of your mother yelling, "I'm not having you washing any more dirty horsy laundry in this household's washing
machine!" Maybe your mom doesn't understand that you can be
responsible about using the family laundry facilities, especially
when you want to do something this important to you. Maybe
she just doesn't like horses, or, underneath her protests, she is
really just worried about your getting hurt. What do you need to
explain to her?

Can you hear your father saying,"Who's going to haul you
back and forth to the barn and to shows and pay the expenses?"
or, if you already have a driver's license, "You're going to end up
using the family car too much of the time. What about your
brother's baseball practices or your little sister's ballet lessons?"
Do you need to discuss a schedule for the use of the family car
and your willingness to exchange some work around the house
for some extra privileges with the car?

Do you envision both of your parents saying, "How will you
have time to do all of this, especially in the late spring, when you
are still in school? How will your school work be affected?" Do
you see yourself having trouble with finding time for school
work, or will you just have to reassure your parents that you can
achieve at school and still show your horse? If you think that
your parents will react negatively, first, think of what objections
they might offer, regarding time, money, school work, and family
schedules, and consider where there could be some reasonable
give and take on both sides. Remember, part of being a family is
caring about each other, so no one family member should be
overly selfish or demanding.

On the other hand, maybe your parents are very positive and
encouraging. That's great, but you must also consider how much
they know about horses. They, too, may be so over eager that
they just don't understand what steps you need to take or why
you can't start competing in the show ring and winning immediately. You may need to explain a lot of horsy ideas to them and
may also need to convince them when it is time to seek out the
advice of a professional. Then, or course, you will need to be
willing to listen when they advise you based on their years' experience just living, dealing with a family and a budget, and making judgments about how other people can help you. Again,
communicating is a two-way street. Sometimes, you may even
need a third party, another adult, who can help you discuss
things with your parents,when you feel not quite adequate in
making an explanation yourself.

One question whose answer may help you focus your need

for time and money in relation to both family and friends is simply what types of shows you will be showing in. Breed association shows can be more expensive than open shows. Shows which require a lot of trailer traveling and overnight accommodations for you and your horse are more expensive than local shows. Parents, relatives, and friends who offer free help make showing less expensive than having to pay someone as a groom or all-around helper.

Now that you have considered why you are showing and have a general idea of what factors may influence your decisions, let's get more specific.

WHAT ARE YOUR ABILITIES AS A RIDER?

The first ability, like it or not, has to do with what we've just been talking about: time and money. If you own a horse now, you or your parents must pay the cost of stabling, veterinarian's services, and farrier (blacksmith) services. Will the family budget be able to handle the added costs of showing fees, showing outfits for you, show tack for your horse, and trailering fees or the cost of a trailer and truck? What sacrifices and compromises must be made by you and the rest of the family? Will you need to get a part time job for added expenses, in addition to doing everything else you already do in your busy life? Will your mom or dad be able to haul you to local horse shows? To overnight shows? Will your parents need to buy a new vehicle to haul a horse trailer? Such a big step may be overdoing it for someone who is just starting out showing. You need to sit down and talk all of these things over with your parents, brothers and sisters, and anyone else involved in your plans. At the end of this chapter, you will find a series of guide sheets on horse care and showing costs and on approximate hours per week needed for horse care and training by the rider, as well as a sample calendar of a typical month's showing activities. See these **3** guide sheets: **Planning a Chart for Horse Care and Training Time; Sample Calendar;** and **Planning for Showing and Trailering Costs.** Use these as guides to create your own plans, and you will have a much more concrete idea of what you can and cannot do in the way of planning for the upcoming show season.

Ok. The next question finally has to do with you as a rider.

OVER THE LONG HAUL, ARE YOU ADAPTABLE TO THE DEMANDS OF HORSE CARE, TRAINING, AND COMPETITION?

WHAT IS YOUR PERSONALITY LIKE?

As a show ring rider, you need to be: **focused, disciplined, dependable, organized, patient, perceptive, open-minded, and able to handle stress associated with managing responsibilities in several areas at once.** That's a tall order. Think it through. Nobody's perfect. What characteristics out of the ones just listed above will you need to work on? What areas will you need to get other people's advice on? Could you talk to some teachers or to a counselor at school for an evaluation of your work habits and interpersonal skills? Could another trusted adult or older rider give you some insight to behavior patterns you demonstrate when you are around horses? Go back over the previous discussion of influences and contributions of parents, neighbors, and friends. How do you deal with problem solving in connection with other people? Are you demanding? Easily led? Scatterbrained? Always making excuses for yourself? Always complaining about other people or about your horse? Wanting results now, no matter what? Do you fall apart easily when demands are made on you? Does every little bang or bruise leave you wanting to give up? Do you get nervous in front of other people? Are you dependable when you promise to do something? Are you noted for your good judgment? Be honest with yourself now. Then, when some little weakness turns up later, and one always does, even for Olympic level contenders, you can whisper to yourself; "Whoops, back up a minute, pal. Let's just stop and think about what works and what doesn't work for me in getting my act together."

Next, what perceptions of yourself as a rider and of your horse as a partner and a performer may you need to rethink in order to reach your goal in the show ring? See the **3** guide sheets at the end of this chapter titled: **Personality Types of Horses and Riders; Schooling Levels of Horses and Riders;** and **Matching Personalities and Schooling Levels of Horses and Riders.** These sheets condense a lot of very important information for you, information that any experienced horseman/woman worth his/her salt will emphasize. Basically, they show you that certain types of rider personalities match better with certain types of horse personalities. Right! If you haven't already noticed, horses have personalities, just like people do. The sheets will show you what kind of rider should be handling what kind of horse that is at any given level of training. The main rules of thumb are:

1)   the more easily frazzled the horse is, the more steady the rider must be; the more easily frazzled the rider is, the more steady the horse must be; and

2)   the less experienced the horse is, the more experienced the rider must be; the less experienced the rider is, the more experienced the horse must be.

A beginning rider will more quickly gain confidence on a wise, old, well-schooled gelding than on a fractious colt. Once the rider has his or her basics down, he or she may advance to a more lively, and therefore more unpredictable mount, and, eventually, to a less fully schooled mount. Don't let anybody tell you that two totally inexperienced (or **green**) companions, you and your horse, will learn the skills together. It doesn't work. It's an accident waiting to happen. (More about evaluating the horse you are planning to show in chapter 2.)

The final step in this chapter on goals is for the rider to ask:

WHAT RIDING AND TRAINING ABILITIES DO YOU, THE RIDER, ACTUALLY HAVE RIGHT NOW?

Refer to the **2** guide sheets at the end of this chapter, titled: **Rider Self-Evaluation of Performance Ability;** and **Questions to Ask a Professional About the Skill and Potential of the Rider and the Horse.** Check to see what skills are beginner, intermediate, and advanced. What skills must a rider have before he can begin to call himself a trainer? Check the **glossary** for words marked * to find explanations of terms you may not fully understand. Tune into yourself as you perform on horseback. Be honest with yourself, and also check among other riders and friends to help you in your self-assessment. (Again, remember to consider the source of any advice offered.) To begin serious preparation for the show ring, in any class above "walk-trot," the rider should be at least intermediate. Make a list, using the guide sheet, of the skills you do and do not know how to perform.

Suppose you decide to seek out a professional instructor or trainer to evaluate you. First, ask around, among other horse professionals, such as trainers, instructors, veterinarians, and blacksmiths, about this person's expertise and reputation. Try to appear neutral about your intentions and listen well. Of course, again, consider the source of your information. If two people are fierce enemies, one is not going to praise the other. If two people are competing for the same customers in the same marketplace, what differences do you notice in what they have to offer? What do their customers say about them? Anyone can hang out a sign to say he or she is a trainer or instructor. How successful he is as a serious horseman depends on his knowledge and his skill with people and horses. These characteristics will be manifested in what he and his customers have achieved in the show ring doing the kind of thing you want to do in the show ring.

Honesty is also an important factor in a business where there is no government regulation on the person claiming to be a professional, next to the normal laws of the land regarding contracts and liability. If all this fellow wants to do for you is sell you one of the horses in his barn the minute you walk onto his place, you may be getting the hustle. If he tells you he can make you a grand champion in thirty days or that one magical bit or training device will solve all of your problems, think again. There's an old saying in the horse business regarding riders and horses: There's no such thing as a thirty-day wonder. Everything takes time, effort, concentration, knowledge, and accumulated experience. Everything. Even fun stuff like riding horses. Most importantly, every horse and every rider must be evaluated as an individual.

When you have decided whom you will seek for a formal evaluation of your skills, refer to the guide sheet mentioned for questions to ask a professional. While he or she is evaluating you, you should also be evaluating him or her regarding time and money involved, should you decide to engage his or her services.

It is also a good idea to take a parent and an adult knowledgeable about horses along with you. If the professional knows about the horse you currently own or are using, this knowledge will be a plus for you, because he will be able to give you some idea about how you and this particular horse will get along working toward the goals you have set for yourself. If he can see you ride on this particular horse, so much the better, because his professional's eye will take in the whole picture of personality and performance level for both horse and rider.

Thus, at this step, you are now ready to consider the points in Chapter two of this book, which center on evaluating your horse. You still have a lot of questions to ask, but you are one step closer to realizing your dream of performing in the show ring.

PLANNING A CHART FOR HORSE CARE
AND TRAINING TIME

MONDAY
This day is usually a rest day, after a weekend's showing or riding activities.

Horse care should include **approximately one hour of grooming time**, to include a cool down after lungeing, if the horse cannot be turned out for free exercise. If the horse is turned out for free exercise for an hour or two, he may need to be hosed off (after he is walked cool first) or vacuumed in cold weather, if he has rolled in dirt.

Horse training time should include only lungeing for exercise, for about **one half hour**, the first fifteen minutes without side reins and the last fifteen minutes with side reins, if needed, but no new routines or excercises should be added to the schedule.

If weather permits, rather than lungeing him, it is preferable that the rider turn the horse out to play and clear his mind.

Other maintenance may include stall cleaning (**fifteen minutes to one half hour,** depending on conditions and services the stable offers), washing water buckets, and cleaning tack, blankets, or saddle pads. Of course, if the horse is turned out to play, the rider may take advantage of time spent at the barn to perform other maintenance chores, while waiting for the horse to finish his play time in the pasture.

TUESDAY
Horse care includes about **one hour of grooming time**, which may be longer, if more time is needed for cooling out the horse in hot weather.

Horse training time includes about **one hour** in the saddle. However, warmup time of fifteen minutes may be done on a lunge line, if the horse is fresh and has not had an opportunity to get out his play to be ready for serious training. After lungeing, the rider should spend approximately one half hour to forty-five minutes on serious training work and the last ten to fifteen minutes on a cool down under saddle. See Chapters 4 through 9 for more specifics. These time limits may vary a little, depending on weather conditions and the personality and training level of the horse.

Other maintenance time may include any mentioned under Monday's schedule, as needed, but must include stall and water bucket cleaning, if not provided by the barn.

WEDNESDAY
Activities will be similar to Tuesday's schedule and may also include an **extra half hour** of riding time for trail riding after the horse's training session.

THURSDAY
This day should be similar to Tuesday and Wednesday's schedules. It may be a day of light training for the horse only if preparation for a show for the weekend includes all day Friday as travel time. A variation may be a day of training or trail riding, followed by some turnout time for the horse, during which the rider prepares for travel to a show. Preparation time may vary, depending upon tack, clothing, and equipment to be hauled, preparation of the trailer, and grooming of the horse. Additional horse care preparations may include bathing the horse, braiding the horse's mane and tail, and/or polishing hooves. The rider must also plan sufficient time to pack necessary tack, clothing, and equipment. If at all possible, he should work the horse under saddle.

FRIDAY
If training is scheduled on Thursday and local hauling to a show, rather than long distance travel, is planned for the weekend, Friday may be the horse's day of rest or light workout, while the rider makes preparations and grooms the horse especially for show ring performance.

SATURDAY and *SUNDAY*
Depending on how many weekends the rider has planned into his showing schedule and depending on his goals for the show season, these days may be spent at horse shows. Otherwise, at least one of these days should be spent on trail riding rather than on schooling the horse, to vary his activity and to prevent him from becoming ring sour at home or in the show ring.

Additional items to schedule: travel to the barn, study time for school work, school activities, job responsibilities, home chores, and casual, non-horsy activities that may be part of a teen's social life.

PLANNING FOR SHOWING AND TRAILERING COSTS
ONE-TIME ITEMS

purchasing the **horse** —   See chapter 2 — at least $2,500 to $5,000

purchasing **horse insurance** — See chapter 2 — $ (annual premium, depending on horse and coverage)

purchasing **tack** —   See chapter 10
    Western saddle,   new, with silver — $
               new, without silver — $
               used, with silver — $
               used, without silver — $

    all-purpose **English saddle,**   new — $
               used — $

    Western bridle,   new, with silver — $
               new, without silver — $
               used, with silver — $
               used, without silver — $

    English bridle,   new — $
               used — $

    Western saddle pad   — $

    English saddle pad   — $

Unless they are in very good condition, it is not recommended that the rider purchase a used pad, as it may be too worn to protect his horse's back properly.

English saddles may be sold with or without fittings, and the cost does not include additional items, like a breastplate. Western saddles do not include the purchase of girth and tie billet or (sometimes) the off billet or extra items, such as a breastplate. All costs are estimates. The rider should spend time pricing items at various tack stores and through catalogs and total up what he can reasonably spend on these items. In Western tack, quality leather and fit are more important than silver.

purchasing the **rider's outfit** — See chapter 10

Western jeans,	new — $	
shirt,	new — $	
chaps,	new, ready-made — $	
chaps,	new, custom — $	
hat, felt,	new — $	
hat, straw,	new — $	
boots,	new, ready-made — $	
boots,	new, custom — $	
gloves,	new, — $	
miscellaneous accessories	— $	
English breeches,	new — $	
blouse or shirt,	new — $	
hunt coat,	new — $	
hard hat,	new — $	
boots,	new — $	
gloves,	new — $	
miscellaneous accessories	— $	

purchasing a **two-horse trailer** — depending on the part of the country and the type and style of trailer, anywhere from

new, — $ to used, — $$

See Chapter 1, for some general suggestions on trailers and trailering

VARIABLE ITEMS

If the rider's horse is being **hauled by a professional,** who carries insurance for this purpose and who trailers others regularly, he may charge the rider a set fee per mile ($2 - $3) (multiplied by number of miles for each show) plus an additional fee for the use of the trailer at the show ring for the day — $

Of course, he may simply drop the rider and horse off at the show ring and pick them up at the end of a day's competition. This arrangement, however, creates the disadvantage of the rider and horse lacking a base of operations for the duration of the day. If the rider can arrange to haul to the show with other competitors, the fee may be reduced, since it will be divided by the number of horses hauled. In addition, the hauler is more likely to agree to park the trailer at the show grounds for the day, since more than one customer is involved.

Another option is to **find a friend who may lend or rent the rider a trailer** for one show or for the show season. Variety in costs of arrangements here are endless.

A third option is for the **friend to do the hauling,** usually for less than a professional hauler may charge. However, insurance may be a problem for hauler and horse owner.

Research into the cost of hauling, multiplied by the number of shows to be attended, will give the rider an idea of how much hauling costs will limit the number of shows he and his horse may attend, in light of funds available.

Employing the regular services of a **veterinarian** (See chapter 3.)
Immunizations: (Check with local veterinarians for fees and farm call charges.)
influenza — $ (check veterinarian in local area for frequency, depending on outbreaks)
rhinopneumonitis — $ (check veterinarian in local area for frequency)
tetanus booster — $ (yearly)
Eastern and Western encephalomyelitis — $ (each spring)
Also check veterinarian for special problems in your area of the country.
coggins test — $ (required before show season)
other, depending on local disease outbreaks and veterinarian's recommendation — $
teeth floating — $ (depending on the horse; check with veterinarian for frequency, but usually at least once a year.)
worming, paste, (every two months) $
worming, tube, including farm call (Check veterinarian's recommendation.) $
emergency fund for accidents, lameness, colic, tying up, and / or other $

Employing the services of a **farrier (blacksmith)** (every month to six weeks, depending on horse's foot growth) (See chapter 3.)
reset existing shoes — $ (Check local blacksmiths' fees)
new shoes — $ (Check local blacksmiths' fees)
corrective shoeing — $ (Check local blacksmiths' fees)
emergency fund for pulled and lost shoes — $

Boarding barn costs — $ (monthly base charge, assuming the horse is not to be kept on the rider's own premises)

Costs will vary drastically from one part of the country to another and depending on whether one is interested in a full-service facility or minimal services. Consider costs in relation to care and expertise of the barn personnel. In milder climates, one may sacrifice the use of an indoor arena for a lower price, but basic care and safety should never be a compromise. (See chapter 3, in horse health care.)

Keeping the horse at home — $ (per month)
    hay — $ (type of hay, per bale, times number of bales, delivered or picked up by horse owner)
    grain — $ (per fifty or hundred pound sack, delivered or picked up by horse owner times number of sacks needed.)
    bedding — $ (in bulk or in bales; wood shavings or straw or other, picked up or delivered, usually measured in cubic yards.)
    stall cleaning help — $ (per hour.)
    maintenance of arena, pastures, buildings, and fencing — $

PERSONALITY TYPES OF HORSES AND RIDERS

RIDER

Type A:
Nervous, timid, but also impatient for desired results. Easily frustrated.

Type B:
Nervous, timid, hesitant, but patient and willing. Not easily frustrated.

Type C:
Confident, patient, and relaxed. A follower who takes direction well.

Type D:
Confident, patient, and relaxed. A leader who also takes direction well.

Type E:
Confident, impatient, take-charge. Often tense without realizing it. Wants quick results. Does not like to accept direction or advice.

Type F:
Over-relaxed and careless about purpose and focus; inconsistent due to lack of attention; having a good time but not serious about work.

HORSE

Type A:
Nervous, timid, high strung. Easily frustrated. Poor concentrator. Either not too smart or so high strung that nervous instinct overcomes thinking and ability to be trained.

Type B:
Nervous, timid, high strung, but a people horse, forgiving and responsive to a patient hand. Intelligence can overcome nervous instincts.

Type C:
Sensitive but not nervous. Confident, forgiving and relaxed. Follows leader's lead. Likes to please. Is at least an average thinker.

Type D:
Sensitive but relaxed and patient. Smart leader type. Often otthinks leader.

Type E:
Tough, bully, impatient. May be smart or stupid, but cheats on rider. Does not respond to aids or to correction well. Unforgiving, stubborn.

Type F:
Relaxed and lazy. Slow-minded. Kind but doesn't care. Sluggish.

SCHOOLING LEVELS OF HORSES AND RIDERS

RIDER

HORSE

A. Beginner: complete novice; neither skilled nor physically fit.

A. Green: completely untrained under saddle; may lead, tie, lunge, and/or ground drive; not physically fit (soft).

B. Novice but able to tack up ride walk and trot under supervision; physical fitness level also needs further development.

B. Trained in basics but inconsistent and undependable; often not yet physically fit enough.

C. Intermediate: able to ride walk, trot, and canter independently, in safe area on safe, schooled horse.

C. Trained for a specific area but with some gaps in training or behavior problems; physically fit for the job.

D. Advanced: able to ride independently at all gaits in open country; may ride problem horses under supervision.

D. Fully schooled in one area or has an all-around mount; very sensitive to rider's aid, but does not make corrections for rider's mistakes.

E. Trainer level: able to ride and school any given mount under any given conditions; also able to diagnose training and behavior problems and affect solutions through good horsemanship.

E. "Broke to Death": fully schooled; completely dependable; sensitive to rider's aids, knows his job, takes care of his rider, and can almost do it on his own.

MATCHING PERSONALITIES AND SCHOOLING LEVELS
OF HORSES AND RIDERS

RIDER		HORSE	
PERSONALITY	SKILL	PERSONALITY	TRAINING

MOST LOGICAL COMBINATIONS:

Type: A through F	A or B	F	E
A or B	C	C or F	E
C or D	C	C, D, or F	E
E	C	F	E
F	C	C or F	E
A	D	C or F	D or E
B	D	C, D, or F	D or E
C	D	A, B, C, D, or F	C,D, or E
D	D	A,B,C,D,E, or F	B,C,D, or E
E	D	C,D, or F	C,D, or E
F	D	C or F	C,D, or E

Note: A rider at trainer level, at **E** level, should either naturally be a **C** or **D** type personality or should have developed his skills to bring out **C** or **D** personality type traits and should have overcome nervousness, insecurity, and impatience. He should have developed a "horseman's eye" and understanding. Thus, a rider at **E** level or skill should be able to handle any type of horse personality at any level of training. Only a rider at trainer level should attempt to school a horse at schooling level **A**.

RIDER SELF-EVALUATION
OF PERFORMANCE ABILITY

BEGINNER LEVEL:

1. cannot handle horse from the ground.
2. cannot tack up or explain use of pieces of tack*.
3. cannot ride independently with control at any gait*.

INTERMEDIATE LEVEL:

1. able to handle schooled horse from ground — grooming, lungeing*, trailer loading.
2. able to tack up horse and identify and explain use of pieces of tack.
3. able to ride walk*, trot, and canter independently in safe area on schooled horse.
    ___ able to attain trot* or jog*;
    ___ able to attain leads* on a canter and attain lope* or canter*;
    ___ able to halt from walk, trot, and canter;
    ___ able to back horse up straight from the ground and under saddle;
    ___ able to attain transitions* from walk to canter and canter to halt, as well as walk to trot and trot to canter, canter to trot, and trot to walk, maintaining balance and proper aids*.
    ___ able to ride a simple lead change* on a figure eight.
    ___ able to ride serpentines at walk and trot.
    ___ able to ride designated size circles at walk, trot, and canter.
    ___ able to ride walk, trot, and canter over cavalletti* and trotting poles.

ADVANCED LEVEL:

1. able to attain extension* and collection* at the walk, trot, and canter.
2. able to ride a flying lead change* through a figure eight.
3. able to perform specialized lateral* moves such as the side pass*.
4. able to ride gymnastic jumping exercises over obstacles up to three feet high.
5. able (with supervision) to correct errors made by the horse and understand principles of diagnosis and correction of specific given training problems.

THE SEARCH FOR THE RIGHT HORSE

In Chapter one, you made a lot of decisions about yourself and your goals. Now, it is time to consider the horse that suits you best in light of those goals, your personality, and your skill as a rider. Remember, however, that just like people, horses are individuals, and none is perfect. In measuring any given horse against the ideal horse, you will more than likely end up making some compromises, regarding conformation, training, temperament (personality), show record, and cost. Once you have read this chapter, you will be better prepared to make wise choices and to judge which areas you can compromise on, while still achieving your show ring goals and enjoying your horse. But what if you don't have a choice of mounts? What if you must deal with the one horse offered to you for lease or the one horse you already own? What if you don't know how to go about leasing a horse? Then, where do you aim in setting your sights for the show ring? This chapter will teach you how to assess the limited options that may be available to you, whether you own or lease. First, however, let's look at the ideal horse.

WHAT ARE THE IDEAL ATTRIBUTES
FOR A SHOW HORSE?

This is a BIG question, so first let's consider general guidelines about **soundness**,* athletic ability (as shown by **conformation***and movement), training level, temperament (personality), show record, and cost. Then, we can consider these factors in relation to the type of classes you and your mount will be showing in and how you can work realistically for success.

Soundness, or overall health, comes first. A lame horse or one with a serious conformation or chronic health problem, which makes him prone to injury in a certain activity, is both a potential danger and an expense in vet bills to have around. (More about health of horse and rider in Chapter 3.) Just as people are advised to check with their doctors before beginning any program of strenuous physical activity — you are preparing two athletes for competition, after all, you and your horse — you should discuss your plans for showing with your veterinarian. He will tell you if your horse will stand up to the program you will set for him or how you might have to modify your training and show routine to safeguard your horse while still working toward your goals in the show ring. (Before buying a horse, you will find a pre-purchase vet exam vital to protecting your interest and your pocket book, but more about this in chapter 12.)

In talking with your vet about a horse you own or plan to own or lease, be frank with your questions and expect frank, direct answers. Like any serious competitor, you need to look at yourself and your horse realistically and honestly, so you may work purposefully toward success. Such levelheadedness on your part may be hard to achieve with friends and family pulling you in many different directions. Thus, you can see how important it is to listen to your veterinarian when you ask those questions and when you have become confused by too much well-intentioned advice from other less-knowledgeable people. Your vet should be the last word when it comes to soundness decisions.

Here are two basic principles to keep in mind about soundness.

1.   A horse with a previous, serious leg injury or a chronic disease must be scrutinized carefully. If, for example, you plan to jump a horse who has an old, healed bowed tendon, you may find that he might not stay sound as a jumper but may work fine in **flat** * classes. Only your vet can say for sure, so have him check the horse out. Then, again, listen to his advice. Don't ignore it, hoping the problem will go away.

Sometimes it's hard to find the courage to face a hard truth. You may need encouragement and consolation from family and friends, if you discover that the horse simply cannot perform as you had hoped he would. However, remember, you don't want to be responsible for causing your horse unneeded pain and risking injury to both of you. You can't sacrifice your safety and your horse's well-being for the sake of the wrong dream.

If, for example, your horse suffers from the disease, **ring-bone***, only a vet's examination and x-rays can say for sure if the horse will be sound and useful at all and for how long. Again, ignoring a serious problem because you hope to win in the show ring is a cruel way to repay a faithful mount who tries to obey your commands and a foolish way to endanger yourself and your horse.

2.   While a horse may move sound and be free from disease, his conformation type may still suggest certain weaknesses and thus indicate precautions, when you are planning training activities for the show ring. For example, a horse with overly long **pasterns***, weak knees, or weak **hocks*** may risk injury from repeated jumping but may perform on the flat satisfactorily. A horse with a shallow hip angle may not do well in Western Horsemanship or in jumping, where his hind quarters must work hard, but he may survive Western Pleasure, English Pleasure, Hunter Under Saddle, and Equitation classes. He may not place as high in pleasure classes as a better balanced horse who looks prettier to a judge, but he will be workable as a first show horse. If his temperament and training are right, he can provide a rider new to showing with a lot of valuable experience.

These are just a few of the problems that you may encounter in judging the horse's suitability for showing. Reading them should have given you some idea of how important evaluating conformation can be before setting show ring goals. Simply put, the rider cannot push the horse beyond what he has the physical ability to achieve without paying sad consequences in injury and vet bills and without ruining the horse's attitude toward his work as well. Who wants to work when he's hurting? So, the next question is what SHOULD you look for in horse conformation? Here are some ideals from head to toe.

HEAD AND NECK:

He should have large, kind, intelligent **eyes** set wide apart for beauty as well as function. A horse with small, "pig" eyes just doesn't see as well. A horse who is narrow between the eyes has less space for his brain and may have a tendency to be stubborn or mean or stupid.

He should have fine alert **ears**, set neither too close nor too wide apart. The tips of the ears of finely bred horses also tend to turn delicately inward, giving the ears an elegant shape. Ears that are too large and coarse are called "mule" ears. While the shape and size of the ears will not affect the horse's athletic ability, they can either add to or detract from his appearance, making him more or less appealing to the eye of the judge in the show ring. The ears are also one indication of the quality of a horse's breeding and the nature of his temperament. Ears that are "on the move" too much may indicate a nervous horse. A horse who lays his ears flat against his head too often may have a nasty nature. A horse who refuses to let you touch his ears may be green (inexperienced and not used to being handled), may have ear mites or some other health problem, or may have had a bad training experience and rough treatment.

He should have full, flexible **nostrils** and a fine **muzzle** with sensitive **lips**. These features also indicate beauty and breeding quality, but generally, a fine muzzle and soft lips also indicate a horse who will be lighter in the bridle and more sensitive to the rider's hands than a coarser horse. Nostrils need to be large for wind capacity.

He should have a deep, full **jaw** line. This feature also adds to beauty and indicates quality in breeding as well.

He should have a clean **throat latch**. This area, where the head joins the neck, is very important. A thick throat latch may be part of a particular horse's natural makeup, but it may also indicate years of poor training which has caused the muscles of the neck in this area to become hard and inflexible. A thick throat latch usually accompanies a thick neck, and this feature means inflexibility and resistance to the rider's hands. Why? If the horse flexes these thick muscles as the rider squeezes on the bridle's reins, the horse's thick neck can actually partly cut off the horse's ability to breathe. How? As he tucks his chin, rounds his neck, and lowers his head, his thick neck may partly cut off his air by restricting his windpipe. What horse would be willing to give to the rider's hands, if he can't breathe when he obeys the command to give? Last, a thick throat latch can also indicate not only training and conformation problems but also personality problems, that is a horse who is stubborn and who is used to resisting his rider and has made a regular habit of doing so, thus developing thick muscles in the underside of his neck.

He should have a **neck** with a graceful arch, neither too long, like a swan, nor too thick and short, like a wrestler. The neck muscles should be developed on the top, not on the bottom, as explained in the above paragraph. A neck which is too "cresty" on top, however, may indicate anything from a naturally heavy, inflexible neck to an overweight horse, or even to a horse who has a glandular health problem. A neck that is too long will allow the horse to snake his head away from his rider very easily. A neck that ties in too low into the chest in the front will inhibit the free flowing movement of the front legs. A neck that goes into the body at the withers at a high angle will mean a naturally high head carriage, making the horse less suitable to Western events and more suitable for English events. An overly high head carriage may make it difficult for the rider to train the horse to relax, reach down and forward, and then round himself and perform "on the bit."* An overly high head carriage combined with a long, flat back can make a horse difficult to ride comfortably, because he is so easily able to raise his head away from the rider's hands and hollow his back away from the rider's seat.

CHEST AND FRONT LEGS:
The chest should be full for large lung capacity but not so large that the horse looks too bulky in front when he is examined from a side view. Sometimes a large chest looks larger because the horse is overweight. In other cases, the horse may simply have weak conformation in his hind quarters or may lack hind quarter development due to poor training or lack of training (he may be young or green). Thus his chest will appear bigger than it should.

The front legs, in relation to the chest, should not look as if they both "came out of the same hole." If they do, the chest is too narrow. This conformation reduces lung capacity and also makes for a horse who lacks flexibility and thus athletic ability. Legs should look "clean" and have a relatively long, straight forearm in relation to a relatively short cannon bone, with large flat knees that allow plenty of room for tendons to tie comfortably into the knee joint. The legs, as a whole, should have enough bone mass to look comfortable supporting the size body the horse has. A horse who is too light-boned will break down more easily and have leg problems in his future. The horse's knees should neither seem to bend backward (calf-kneed) nor bend forward (over at the knee). Weak knees, of course, limit athletic ability in horses just like they do in people. Pasterns* should be long and sloping without being so long as to affect the stability of the suspensory ligament. Pastern angle should match hoof angle. A mismatch means either that the horse had a bad shoeing job done on him or that he has overly long, weak pasterns, which could mean too many sprains and strains, when the horse is put to serious work. Pasterns that are too steep and straight, on the other hand, not only make for a choppy stride and a bumpy ride for the rider but also make the horse prone to navicular disease* and ringbone.*

SHOULDER, BARREL, BACK, AND HINDQUARTERS:
The horse's shoulder angle should match his hip angle. Too steep an angle indicates a horse with a jarring stride and one who will not have the flexibility and extension ability of a better athlete, whose angles are more sloping. Both shoulder and hip should be

full and well-developed, whether the horse is a long, slender-muscled type (like a thoroughbred) or the football player type (like the quarter horse).

The horse's barrel, or rib cage area, should be deep and full to match his chest. His ribs should be well-sprung for good lung capacity. The withers above the chest should be defined enough to support a saddle. Too flat a withers (called "mutton withered") not only means less flexibility in the shoulder area but also means that this horse will have a hard time keeping a saddle centered when going around corners and when traveling up and down hills. The saddle will slip and slide all over the place.

The horse's back should be short and strong, not long and sagging (called "swayback"), a definite weakness and one which makes it difficult for the horse to collect himself and get his hindquarters under himself to maneuver safely and gracefully. His top line, from withers to tail, viewed from the side, should be short in relation to his underline, from front legs to back legs.

His hindquarters should be strong and angled in harmony with his shoulder. His hip angle should tie in strongly, with well-developed muscles through his gaskins* and down into his hind legs. His tail, for beauty's sake, should be set on neither too high nor too low, and his croup* should not be too steep, as this affects the angle and depth of the hip. The horse, as a whole, should not appear to be higher in back than he is in front, because such a build makes it difficult for him to get his weight off his front end (forehand) and get his hindquarters under him (engage his hindquarters) to work properly with a rider on his back.

Last, his hind legs should have the same quality of bone and muscle as his front legs. His hocks* should be clean and well-developed with space for tendons to tie into the joint. His hocks should make the legs have a pleasing angle, so that he does not look like he is about to sit down or, on the other hand, like he has camped his hind legs out behind himself. If his hocks look like they will knock together when he is viewed from behind, this joint and the whole back leg is weak and will not stand up under hard work. Pastern angle on the hind legs is always a little steeper than on the front legs, but again, the angle of the pastern should match the angle of the hoof.

HOOF:
The old horseman's saying,"no foot, no horse," holds true. The horse should have well-shaped hooves that are big enough to carry his weight and bone size but not so pie-plate big that they make him look clumsy and fumble-footed. A mule-footed shape

can simply mean the horse has had a bad blacksmith job or that the horse's hooves are naturally shaped like a mule's. This shape, more like a narrow oval than a full one, may mean contracted heels or future navicular or ringbone disease problems, because the internal structures of the hoof do not have enough space to expand as the horse puts his weight on his hoof in taking a step. The outer surface of the hoof should be smooth and consistent in color. Some people say that white hooves tend not to be as strong as gray hooves, but the overall hoof health should be the focus of concern. Deep rings around the outer surface of the hoof, sometimes called "fever rings," can mean a history of illness in the past year such as laminitis*. A hoof with deep cracks or grooves may mean previous injury, poor hoof quality that will not stand up to stress, poor nutrition, or breakdown from the horse being worked regularly on too hard a surface. A hoof that seems to be riddled with old nail hole marks from past shoeing may indicate that the horse has weak hoof walls and has difficulty keeping shoes on or that the horse has a chronic lameness problem that only very frequent shoeings can keep in check. Viewed from the bottom, the sole of the hoof should appear firm, and the triangular-shaped frog* should appear healthy and flexible, a little like firm rubber. The sole should not appear "dropped" or sunken, a dangerous sign of previous founder*.

With all of the above conformation ideals in mind, the next question is, of course:

WHAT ARE THE MOST IMPORTANT CONFORMATION POINTS TO LOOK FOR IN A HORSE YOU WOULD LIKE TO SHOW IN A SPECIFIC SHOW RING CLASS, AND HOW DO THESE POINTS AFFECT THE HORSE'S MOVEMENTS OR ATHLETIC POTENTIAL FOR THAT CLASS?

WESTERN
Western Pleasure:
This horse ideally has an attractive head, a clean throat latch that allows the horse to flex his neck and lower his head so that it is almost level with his withers, a neck which comes out of his body horizontally, a short back, strong, balanced muscling in shoulders and hindquarters, and legs that swing forward low to the ground without a lot of knee or hock action. He is able to keep this easy "low-to-the-ground" shape or "frame," using his strong hindquarters and hind legs to reach under himself softly without raising his forehand (front end), as he strides along in slow, gentle gaits.

Western Horsemanship

This horse may have the eye-pleasing look of the pleasure horse, but he may be build a little more upright, and his gaits may be acceptable with a little more knee and hock action, but not much. When he uses his strong hindquarters to reach under himself, his forehand may come up a little, so that he is rounded in a little higher arc. His gaits may have a little more energy and vertical spring, but he should not look like he is stepping to a marching band.

Representative Western Pleasure Quarter Horse type conformation, rider attire, and riding form.

ENGLISH

Hunter under saddle:

This horse needs an attractive head and a clean throatlatch that allows him to flex his neck and lower his head, but his neck may arc a bit higher than the Western horse's. His strong, short back and well-muscled, balanced shoulders and hind- quarters give him power, but his muscles are long and slender, and although his stride may sweep low, he has more spring and extension in his long, reaching movements.

Representative Hunter Under Saddle Quarter Horse type conformation, rider attire, and riding form.

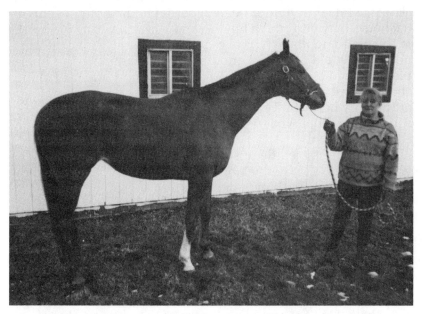

Representative Hunter Under Saddle thoroughbred type conformation.

Hunt seat equitation:

This horse may have the eye appeal of the English horse just de-scribed, but his neck can come out of his chest at a little steeper angle, and his gaits, like the Western horsemanship candidate, may be acceptable with a little more knee and hock action, but not much. When he uses his hindquarters to reach under him-self, his forehand may come up a little more, so that he, too, is rounded in a little higher arc than the English horse described for hunter under saddle. His gaits too may have a little more energy and vertical spring, but, again, he should not look like he is step-ping to a marching band.

To help you develop a horseman's eye in evaluating a horse's conformation and how it affects his movement and, thus, his athletic ability, let's practice by looking at a few photographs. There are four basic conformation types: the long, slender-mus-cled thoroughbred type; the long, slender saddlebred type; the heavier muscled Quarter horse type; and, the heavier muscled carriage horse type. The thoroughbred type and the Quarter horse type are the two which you will find most useful as show horses for the classes in which you are now planning to compete, although the thoroughbred type will be suited only for English classes, while the Quarter horse type, depending on the individ-ual horse, may perform in English and Western. Study the horses in the photographs as typical examples of the style of conforma-tion you would normally choose. When examining the horses pictured, remember: you will find both good and bad things about almost any individual horse, no matter what general type or category his overall conformation may be. The idea is to make a judgment about what type of show ring activity he is best suit-ed for.

If you are still a little unsure about your expertise in judging your own horse's potential for performance in a particular show ring event, you have plenty of company. Developing an "educat-ed" horseman's eye takes time and patience watching many horses' performances. Before you let discouragement block out your desire to achieve, remember, each horse and each rider is an individual, and the whole team is greater than the sum of its sep-arate parts.

The easiest way to gain a sense of perspective about confor-mation and movement and to restore your confidence is to get some help. Don't take on the burden of the decision about your horse's suitability for showing all alone. Ask your veterinarian, your blacksmith, and other experienced horsemen and horsewomen whom you trust for their objective, honest opinions. Then, write down your horse's strengths and weaknesses in light of what you have learned. Then, wait a day or two before you go back to examine what you have written. This waiting will give your mind time to digest everything you have read here and everything you have been told by others. While you are waiting, make a point of watching how your own horse moves freely in his pasture. Watch other horses moving at liberty or under saddle. Think; watch; consider. Then, go back to your written description, and you will have a better, more "educated" perspective on what you can do with your own mount.

Armed with the above information, you are now ready to start putting some more pieces of the puzzle together.

HOW DO CONFORMATION, LEVEL OF TRAINING, TEMPERAMENT OR PERSONALITY, AND SHOW RECORD DETERMINE THE HORSE'S SUITABILITY FOR SHOWING UNDER A CERTAIN RIDER (YOU), AND HOW DOES ALL OF THIS ADD UP TO THE BOTTOM LINE, COST?

Now is the time to go back to those charts in chapter 1:

PERSONALITY TYPES OF HORSES AND RIDERS; SCHOOLING LEVELS OF HORSES AND RIDERS; and MATCHING PERSONALITIES AND SCHOOLING LEVELS OF HORSES AND RIDERS.

The prettiest horse with the most fluid movement will do you little good, if his training is not at the level you can handle or if you and he clash in personality. Examine the charts carefully. Find the ideal personality and training level for your personality and riding ability. Then, see where the compromises must be made in conformation and athletic ability, for you have to be able to handle your mount and get along with him before you can plan on going one inch farther. Again, remember, no rider and no horse will be absolutely perfect. The final judgment call will be yours. Make it the best one you can and move forward. You may need to revise your plan of action a bit as you work with your horse, but trust yourself. You have done a lot of work and thinking so far, hopefully with the help of some very good people.

As one last step before thinking about cost, let's look at some hypothetical cases of riders like yourself.

Let's take Sam, a relatively tall, long-legged, athletic young man of 16, who wants to show Pancho, a big, 12-year old dun Quarter horse gelding in Western Pleasure classes in open shows. Sam has the length of leg and is fit enough to ride big, strong, fast Pancho. Pancho has spent most of his life owned and ridden by an amateur barrel racer, Andy, who loved to compete. Andy found that Pancho had often been coming up sore in his hocks after shows during the last show season, so Andy decided to sell Pancho and get a younger mount to compete on.

Sam bought Pancho for $5000, figuring that the hock problem would disappear if the horse were shown in pleasure classes exclusively, since these classes do not make the demands for the hock straining, high speed and tight turns that barrel racing requires. Sam is bold and athletic, not intimidated by speedy Pancho, who is used to racing and who even likes to bolt around the show ring. All Sam needs to do is re-school (retrain) Pancho, so that Pancho will perform for pleasure classes. Simple enough, right? Whoa! Not so fast.

First, Sam should have had a vet perform a pre-purchase exam on Pancho to determine the exact nature of his hock problem. Is it just minor strain from stress? Is it a combination of stress and weak conformation? Is it the early symptoms of dangerous hock disease that could limit his years of usefulness as a performance horse?

Second, what about Sam's ability and experience as a trainer and his patience to work through the slow, careful process of retraining a horse who is mature and set in his ways into one pattern of performing? If Sam has a lot of experience and patience or some experience plus the help of a very experienced horseman or a trainer, Sam may change Pancho's way of going. This process could take from several months to a year, depending on Sam and on Pancho. If Pancho's personality, however, is such that he is just too hot to be a pleasure horse, or if Pancho is a bit bull-headed as well, Sam may never end up with a satisfactory pleasure horse.

If Sam has enough experience and or help, he might be better off spending his $5000 and that schooling time working a younger horse, who is more sound, who is not set in his ways, and who may have a personality more suited to Western Pleasure. If Pancho is sound physically but needs a lot of retraining and if it looks like he will be trainable, perhaps he might work out. Since he needs retraining, however, Sam might have offered less than $5000 for him. If Pancho has a soundness problem, he may not be worth buying at any price, because he will never be able to do what Sam wants him to do. That's a lot to consider, isn't it? Whatever Sam finds out and whatever he finally decides to do, he will have to make some compromises somewhere. But, then again, many horse deals require some type of compromise, because it is rare to find the perfect horse at a price affordable to a rider just beginning to work into showing.

Second, let's look at Julie, age 14. She too is athletic, plays tennis, and swims, but she is not very tall. Although she has relatively short legs, she is reasonably strong and fit. She just started riding a year ago and loves horses. She is both kind and patient. Her inexperience, however, makes her a bit timid at the canter and hand gallop, although she doesn't like to admit her riding level is only intermediate. She wants to advance quickly. She is leasing a friend's old, steady, dependable, grade* mare, Peggy, and Julie's confidence is beginning to grow, so much that Peggy's steady temperament is beginning to bore Julie.

Julie wants a horse of her own to show Hunter Under Saddle and eventually to graduate from flat classes to those over fences. Moon Night, a shiny, black, three-year-old, thoroughbred filly just off the race track has come to Julie's attention. Julie's in love at first sight. When she hears that the price is only $2000, she dreams of making Moon Night the best hunter in the area. Her mind fills with images of show ribbons, as she watches the filly "fly" around the pasture. She laughs at the filly's antics, as the horse shies at every strange noise and goes darting off, tail held high. When Julie tries the filly under saddle, however, she is secretly grateful that she had gotten on the horse in an indoor ring, for she couldn't control the filly's speed or her spooking. Julie's legs don't seem long enough for her to feel secure in the saddle, and she can't quite figure out why she's having so much trouble. Didn't the filly love to be petted and fed carrots in her stall? Weren't they going to be friends? Julie was sure she had touched a kindred spirit in this fiery, black creature. Julie's friends encourage her, saying that the filly just has to get to know her and that she will never be able to find such a beautiful animal again at such a reasonable price. Julie is torn. What to do?

First, what about that pre-purchase vet exam to find out if the horse has any physical problems? Second, what about the filly's training and handling history? Why is she so spooky? Did anything bad happen to her on the track? What is her conformation like? Will she be suitable as a hunter in movement? Will she grow to be calm and dependable? A very experienced horseman or trainer needs to evaluate this situation. If the filly has potential and is truly a bargain, Julie really should consider showing Peggy for one season, so she can develop her own horsemanship and experience, while Moon Night is being professionally trained. Then, with supervision, Julie and Moon Night can show next year, when Julie is more experienced and has had a chance to grow a little taller, so that her legs will be a little longer. Julie's bound to get hurt as well as ruin Moon Night's training, if she tries to take on this challenge alone.

Next, let's take a look at Jennifer. She's not very strong athletically, but she loves to ride when she can take a lesson or borrow a friend's well-schooled mount. She wants to show both English and Western and knows she should start out with pleasure classes first. She wants a horse that can do everything and take her far, but her parents don't have the money either to buy her an expensive, high-powered show horse or to let her attend as many shows as she would like to. Her limit has been set at $2500 for the horse and only $500 for all showing this season. Since she is turning sixteen soon, she plans on getting a part time job and saving her money, so that next year she will be able to attend more shows.

She comes across Apple Pie, a mostly Quarter horse gelding, who is sound, eight years old, and who has been shown successfully for two seasons in 4-H shows, mostly Western. Apple is willing to do anything for his rider, but he moves with only average athletic ability, tends to do better in Western than English classes, and though not unbalanced in conformation or general appearance, is just not fancy enough for Jennifer's hopes and dreams. The asking price is $3000, but the owner might take the $2500 she has, maybe. Should she wait for something better to come along? Should she keep riding her friends' horses, while she saves her money for a fancier horse? Is she willing to sell this horse later, when her experience and athletic development warrant moving up to a more expensive mount? After the horse has passed a pre-purchase vet exam and after she has tried him out under English and Western tack and after she has gotten the opinions of some experienced horseman about how they look together as a team, she should decide. Then, she should think about how that part time job she plans to get will affect her time for school work and for riding. It's never as simple as it looks at first, is it? And, it seems that we can never have everything we want right away? But then, that's what compromise and decision making are all about, isn't it?

Last, let's take a look at Mike. For his seventeen years, he has the savvy of an experienced adult horseman. Why? He has spent every summer since he was twelve working for a professional trainer and saving his money. He wants to find a young horse that he can show at open shows this season, to "put some miles" on him. Then, he plans to begin competing in registered Quarter horse shows and begin making his mark as an up and coming trainer in the horse industry, starting next season.

He runs across Amber, an appendix registered, chestnut Quarter horse filly, who is only "just coming" three years old, but who is well-bred and both sound and the prettiest mover he has seen in a long time. Her appendix registry means she will be a little hot to handle, and since she is young, green, and unproven, he thinks he can get her for $6500. If she passes the pre-purchase exam and if he gets along with her under saddle, should he buy her? More than likely, he will say yes. He has both the experience and the desire to handle her right. She has the potential to provide what he needs. He's the type of person who can buy for bloodlines and put much of a horse's training on a green horse himself, without ruining the horse's mind or body. A less experienced person would be unwise to go for this deal without professional help.

While all of the above hypothetical cases may pose some very realistic situations, none of them will match yours exactly. That is why you must make the final decisions about showing a particular horse based on your thorough analysis of your own current situation. Well, what if the worst happens? What if you decide that the horse you own or would like to show is not the right candidate for the job? Do you give up? Not hardly. You really want to do this showing thing, don't you? Well, then, let's look at another possibility: leasing.

Even if you own a horse which you do not plan to show, if you have a little extra money and a little extra time to handle a second horse on a limited basis, you might want to lease a show horse, until you can afford to buy a horse more suited to showing. If you don't own a horse at all and can't see your way clear to buy anything even close to what you need for showing, you still might be able to find a horse to lease.

SO, HOW DO YOU GO ABOUT LEASING?

What are the legal problems you may encounter? The expenses? It would seem that when two adults get together to make a deal about one person using something that belongs to the other, like a house or apartment, they may agree to do whatever they mutually decide is fair. Right? Well, yes, but it's not quite that simple, especially with a living "piece of property," the horse. Besides, if you are under age 18, you are not an adult, and it will be your parents who have to sign an agreement to lease. Who knows what's fair? Who knows what's legal? Tough questions, but they are not impossible to answer. Following the two major steps below will save you a lot of hassles and should result in a safe, satisfying, and affordable agreement.

First, take care to answer all of the following questions. What do you plan to do with the horse compared to what the owner plans to let you do with the horse? Make a list and compare ideas and make compromises where necessary. Will you ride on the barn's premises and at shows? Which shows? Can you use the horse to trail ride? Who will haul the horse to shows? Can you have helpers? Who? Only selected people will be allowed to handle the horse, for safety and insurance reasons, so specify who and make sure there is clear agreement. Who will carry the insurance policy? You will probably need some type of insurance. Whose tack and equipment will be used? Any specifications on these items? Any items of tack which the horse will not tolerate or which he is not used to? Any particular behavior problems or vices peculiar to this horse? Any health problems or special care instructions? Who pays the horse's board, shoeing, and vet bills or what per cent of them? Which days of the week may you use the horse, if the lease is to be partial and not a full lease? Will the stable where the horse is boarded require a special release form for a non-owner to handle the horse on the stable's premises? What about riding lessons or sessions with a trainer? Will the horse's owner approve of your choice of instructor or trainer? Why or why not? How long will the lease last? One month? All summer? Longer? How will the money be paid to the owner? Monthly? All of these questions must be answered fully before an official agreement can be drawn up. Does that mean a formal agreement? Yes, that's step two.

Second, the safest thing to do in a lease agreement is to get an attorney to write up the conditions you agreed on in #1 above into a formal lease that covers a specific amount of time. Then, your parents and the horse's owner will sign and the horse's owner and you will know the limits, feel legally bound, and know what each side must live up to. If this sound like a serious commitment, it is, so it ought to be done right. Such an agreement will save a lot of heart ache and frazzled nerves later, if something goes wrong. Remember the old saying: plan for the worst and expect the best.

One last possibility. What if you own a horse who is not suited to showing and you decide to sell him and buy a different mount? That topic will be covered in chapter 12: **DECIDING TO SELL: MOVING UP OR MOVING OUT.** For now, let's take a look at the next topic for consideration: the health of horse and rider, found in chapter 3.

GETTING IN SHAPE FOR COMPETITION:
The Physical and Mental Health of Horse and Rider

Now that you have chosen your horse and decided on a basic plan for achieving your goals, you must consider one more very important issue before you begin your training routine: health. Who ever heard of any athlete competing if he wasn't in shape for his sport? If he's foolish enough to try without preparing his body and mind, he has doomed himself to failure and maybe even injury before he has even begun. Your final step, then, before plunging into that training program, will be to assess both yourself and your horse in some very specific ways. First, let's take a look at you, the rider.

HOW DOES THE RIDER DETERMINE HIS PHYSICAL FITNESS LEVEL FOR THE SPORT OF RIDING, AND HOW DOES HE ENSURE A SUFFICIENT FITNESS LEVEL FOR RIDING?

Analyzing the complexities of physical fitness programs designed by physicians who are experts in sports medicine goes far beyond the scope of this handbook. What this book can help you to assess, though, is your basic fitness level for training and competition in the Western and English show ring classes on which this book centers. It can get you thinking about your strength, flexibility, and endurance. It can also help you to keep yourself fit enough to ride without constant discomfort and threat of injury from doing the work at hand.

First, take an honest look at yourself. Are you a couch potato who gets out of breath just climbing a flight of stairs? Are you an average person who gets moderate physical exercise in his daily activities and considers riding as his main sport? Are you the "jock" type involved intensively in other sports besides riding? Is your weight a problem? Do you have old injuries from participating in other activities or from whatever? Do you have any congenital problems like curvature of the spine or bad knees? Do you have breathing problems like asthma? After you have had a "heart-to-heart" talk with yourself, make a list of the things you find easy and hard to do related to riding, such as: lifting a Western saddle onto the back of a horse; maintaining a trot or canter around the arena for however many revolutions before you are tired and lose your balance and control; shoveling out a stall; or grooming a horse for show. Be honest with yourself, especially if an action causes you pain or brings on a sense of panic that you are so tired that you cannot control your body's movements or your horse.

Now, take yourself and that list to your doctor and have a physical exam and a "heart-to-heart" talk with him about what you are planning to do for show ring competition. Take your parents or another trusted adult along with you to listen, help ask questions, and to pick up on the doctor's suggestions you may miss or misunderstand. Be sure to share your ideas with these adults before and after the doctor's visit, so you will know how to approach each item you may have a question about. Then, listen to and act on your doctor's advice. Make notes if you have to. What does the doctor say about your plans for regular training workouts with your horse, for regular activities of horse care, and for a planned schedule for competition? Where does he place you in fitness level in strength, flexibility, and endurance? What does he suggest you do to improve or maintain your current level of fitness? What warnings, if any, does he give you about potential injury for your body type or your health history? At his suggestion, you may even need to contact a local university sports medical center or a sports rehabilitation therapist to plan your physical activities, if you have a special problems. Better safe than sorry later.

Okay, now that you have assessed your condition physically, what's the second step? The basic answers are: cross training, vigilance, and common sense warmups. Fortunately for today's rider, there are many excellent books and video tapes on the market which provide specific workout routines for the rider concerned about his overall fitness for the sport. These center around stretching techniques (on and off the horse) to develop flexibility; aerobic activity (such as running, walking, biking, or "jazzercise," to build endurance; and weight lifting (for conditioning and strength, not for power and bulk). Whatever routine you and your doctor decide is ultimately suited to your needs, remember you must work out at least three times per week.

If this sounds like a lot of bother and nothing to do with riding, keep in mind what your sport will demand of you. You must be supple and flexible in the saddle. Your lower back and seat must be able to follow your horse's movements. Your shoulders must be relaxed. Your legs must be able to "grow long" from the inside of your thighs at the crotch all the way down your leg. Your hamstrings must be flexible enough to let your heel naturally hang lower than your toes. You must be strong enough to maintain the correct position in the saddle at all gaits for as long as the judge will take to evaluate your class in the show ring. Your endurance, balance, and coordination cannot fail you, if your horse becomes excited and gives you a hard time or if you must make one more long trip around the arena at the canter or lope in proper form. You see, it's very important that you plan now to allow time for that routine of physical activity which prepares you to work as a rider. As the body builders say: "Just do it!" Think enough of yourself and what you plan to do with your horse to make that time to work on your own body three times per week. Your VIGILANCE and effort in this CROSS TRAINING activity will improve your performance ability as a rider.

Third, make sure that every day when you plan to climb into that saddle that you allow yourself at least ten minutes of stretching exercises on the ground first. Runners and dancers warm up beforehand, don't they? Okay, then take a few minutes to do some simple things. This is your WARMUP for riding. Be sure to breathe deeply and slowly as you perform this routine. Stand with your feet together, hands at your sides. Raise your arms above your head and stretch tall. Then, touch your toes a few times, slowly letting your hamstrings and butt muscles stretch. Next, with your feet about two and one half feet apart, tuck your seat under you and keep your shoulder square, as though you were in the saddle. Bend first your right knee slowly, keeping your left leg straight, stretching your inner left thigh. Then, switch to bending your left knee and stretching your right inner thigh. Next, stand like a swordsman in a lungeing stance, with your hands on your hips, right foot forward. Bend your right knee, keep your back straight, and keep your butt under you. Let your left leg stretch out behind you, stretching your hamstrings. Then, switch legs. This exercise improves leg strength and balance as well as preparing you to be flexible in the saddle.

Another good stretching exercise for your warmup is the torso twist. Stand with your feet about two feet apart and with your arms out at your sides, like airplane wings. Keeping everything below your waist facing forward, slowly twist your arms and torso one half turn to the left. Then, come back to a forward stance. Then, slowly twist your torso to the right. You will find that your waist and back stretch out and loosen up. You can use one arm at a time to loosen up your shoulders and arms in yet another exercise. Stand tall and slowly make circles with your arm, letting your shoulder rotate and stretch.

Last but not least, loosen up your neck by standing tall and simply tilting your head slowly forward while keeping the rest of you straight. Then, tilt your head to the left and try to touch your ear to your shoulder. Then, do the same on the right. With this simple warmup, you will be doing for yourself what you do for your horse when you put him on the lunge line before you work him under saddle. You may also find, surprisingly, that your mind, just like your horse's, will also be more focused on the work at hand, as your tensions melt away and your muscles stretch out.

Whatever you do, pay attention to your own posture and way of walking at all times, to build your rider's posture and grace of movement. Always walk tall, with shoulders square, hanging naturally, and with your butt under you. Don't be stiff, but treat your body like the athlete you expect it to be. Walk by swinging your leg freely from your hip, not baby-stepping along from your knees or slumping over like a very old person. Keep your head up, chin level, and be proud of who you are. Let your arms swing freely and naturally as you walk. Develop the posture and confidence of a competitor. You are what you imagine and work yourself into being. Respect that self and expect something out of it. Pay attention to your need for rest and for a proper diet. If you don't take care of your body, it won't be able to perform well for you, no matter what else you may do. It will give out in a pinch, and you may be injured.

So much for the physical fitness end of things. Now for the next question about the rider. You have probably seen this one coming.

HOW DOES THE RIDER'S FRAME OF MIND AFFECT HIS ABILITY TO WORK WITH HORSES?

Positive imaging, as described above in the discussion on physical fitness, can do a lot to help you mold your attitude about yourself, your self-image. Other factors, though, besides your own perceptions, can affect your ability to concentrate and perform and your ability to handle your horse. Start taking notice of the stresses in your life. We all have them: the boy friend who's always late picking you up for school; the little brother or sister who is a royal pain; the term paper that is due in just five days. Seek out counselors or teachers at school or other adult friends or family or a clergyman if you have a serious problem at hand. Don't try to carry it around by yourself. It will eat you up inside, and you will find yourself unable to concentrate and unable to be patient with your horse. Such careless lack of patience could mess up his training. Worse, it could get both of you hurt. You are the one in charge of him, so you have to be smarter than he is, remember? You have to read him and his needs. You have to be in control of yourself. Make a point of leaving the day's tensions and stresses behind when you arrive at the barn. Use your stretching warmup to clear your mind as well as your body of "bad vibes."

Remember also, that large, beautiful animal that you expect so much of has the mind of a three-year-old child, with the attention span to match. Take a little time sometime and watch the behavior of preschool children. How long can they concentrate on one thing? Now think of your horse. He can be very smart, even crafty, but he is a basic thinker who can concentrate on only one thing at a time for only a short time, maybe five minutes, and he is easily distracted. His attention span may be short, but he does have an excellent memory and responds well to rewards, consistency, and patience. The smarter he is the more variety he enjoys in his work, so he doesn't become bored. He needs to be corrected immediately and appropriately for a mistake or a refusal. He's like a child. You are like his parent or teacher. If your head isn't on straight, don't expect him to fix things for you. If you bring tensions and anger to the barn, he cannot understand and say, "Oh, I'm sorry you're upset. I'll be extra good for you today." More than likely, he will sense that something is wrong with you and will pick up on your bad vibes, acting worse than usual, because he can't understand what's setting you off. He may become upset at every little thing and seem to forget the most basic things you have taught him. Thus, you both become an accident waiting to happen. And it will be your fault, not his, if something goes wrong. You are in charge, remember? Don't let disaster happen to you. Start paying attention to yourself and developing the habits of a sensible horseman, one with self awareness who thinks before he acts and who reads the reactions of his horse.

Such self perception becomes especially important when you face the "show ring jitters" before competition, the euphoria after winning or placing in a class, or the letdown that comes with defeat. Before you let yourself react, take note of how your behavior will affect your horse and other riders around you. If you need to talk something over, do it quietly with someone who knows what you are about. Never take temper tantrums and NEVER, NEVER take anything out on your horse! Would you beat your child if you had an argument with your spouse or neighbor? All this advice is not meant to make you paranoid but rather to make you aware of yourself and how your behavior affects your horse's.

The second major issue at hand in this chapter is, of course, the health of your mount.

HOW DOES THE RIDER DETERMINE HIS HORSE'S PHYSICAL FITNESS LEVEL, AND HOW DOES THE RIDER MAINTAIN IT?

Once again, the first stop on this one is your veterinarian. Keep you horse on a regular schedule of inoculations and worming, according to your veterinarian's advice, to make sure your horse is healthy enough to be worked regularly under saddle. See the list of inoculations in chapter 1, Guide Sheet #2, **Planning for Showing and Trailering Costs,** the section on employing the regular services of a veterinarian. Keep accurate records not just for your horse's sake, but also because you will not be allowed to compete in the show ring without this important information up to date, especially the results of a yearly coggins test.

While you are at it, have your veterinarian assess your horse's general fitness level and soundness, so that you may have a clear idea of where to start his training. How many minutes per day can you work him at the start? Are there any limitations on what you can or cannot do with your horse? For example, if he is very "soft," that is, out of shape, or very young, should you work him only thirty minutes at a time the first week and only at the walk and trot? Can you ride him out on the trail up and down hills? Is he recovering from an injury, like a sprained stifle* for example, which would limit working him on hills or in small circles for a time? Ask specific questions based on what you know about the horse's health history. Write down the advice the veterinarian gives you. Adjust your training program in accordance with the vet's advice.

Your next stop is the blacksmith or farrier. Consult with him about the type of shoes your horse needs, how often he needs to be reset, and the condition of his hooves. If he has soft, sensitive feet, he may bruise his soles easily and may need some special pads. If his feet are dry and brittle, he may need a feed supplement and some extra care by the blacksmith and you to get his feet in shape for competition. Keep a record of his shoeing schedule and needs.

Speaking of food supplements, the next thing you must do, of course, is to pay careful attention to your horse's diet. Your veterinarian, your blacksmith, and your feed store owner can all help you to determine what type of feed and how much feed your horse should have daily and if any special vitamin or mineral supplements are needed. (It is wise to have the vet check the horse's teeth to be sure that he is able to chew his food properly and that he does not need sharp edges on his teeth filed, that is "floated.") What type of grain should he have? Straight oats? Sweet feed? What percentage of protein should he be on? Too high a percentage can lead to a horse who either has so much energy that he wants to jump out of his skin or to a horse who becomes afflicted with painful laminitis and sometimes fatal founder*. What about hay? Timothy? Alfalfa? Orchard grass? A mix? Some horses do fine on alfalfa, while other horses colic on so rich a hay. Remember also, that something can be taken out of a horse's diet suddenly, but anything that is added must be done gradually, so that the horse's sensitive digestive system doesn't become upset and cause him to colic*. Keep him on a regular schedule. Ideally, he should be fed at least three times a day, at the same times each day. Some horses get very upset, can lose weight from worry, or can even colic if their feeding schedule is severely disrupted. Also be sure that you have an experienced person teach you to distinguish types of grain and hay and to detect if a bale of hay or a container of grain is moldy. Even a little mold can kill a horse. Don't ever let anyone get careless with your horse's feed or tell you that it's only a little bad. Who ever heard of a horse who was "just a little dead"?

Next, have someone who is more experienced than you examine your saddle and bridle while they are on your horse. Do they fit properly? Is the bit adjusted properly in the horse's mouth, not too high or too low? Does the bit fit, or is it too large, sliding around in the mouth, or too small, pinching the corners of the horse's mouth? Is the tree of the saddle the correct width, neither too wide nor too shallow? Are the bars of the saddle tree the correct length? An Arabian needs a saddle tree with bars that are shorter than a Quarter horse needs. A thoroughbred will wear a tree that is narrower than the tree for a Quarter horse's saddle.

Last, you need to consider one more important question, before you plunge into your training program:

HOW DOES THE RIDER DETERMINE THE HORSE'S MENTAL FITNESS, AND HOW DOES THE RIDER MAINTAIN A PROPER ATTITUDE IN HIS HORSE FOR WORK?

First, go back to the charts in chapter one: **Guide Sheet #3: Personality Types of Horses and Riders; and Guide Sheet #4: Schooling Levels of Horses and Riders.** Remember generally that even a bright, intelligent horse has the attention span of a three-year old human child along with tremendous physical energy and power. You must teach him discipline and control without bullying him or scaring him. You must also remember to reward him immediately when he does well with a pat and a "good boy!" You must punish him simply and quickly right after he does wrong. One simple, direct, "Quit!" or one tap with a dressage whip behind your leg as you sit in the saddle will do much more good than pulling and yanking on the reins, yelling at the top of your lungs, and repeated whacks with a whip.

Go back and look at how you assessed your horse's personality and behave accordingly around him. If he's nervous, you will have to be very patient and calm. If he is deliberately slow and stubborn, you may have to be more firm and insistent. Observe his reactions to your commands and adjust your body aids and your voice cues appropriately. Moreover, you want your horse to continue to build his concentration level and his confidence and willingness to perform for you, as well as his physical ability to do so. Therefore, you must give him breaks between training activities. If you work on something for ten or fifteen minutes, let him relax under saddle or on the lunge line (however you may be working him at the time) before you go on to your next routine. Don't demand too much of him at once, pushing at him and repeating a move over and over and over until he rebels or gets bored to death. Don't demand that he do too many things in one training sessions either. You will confuse him, and he will either rebel or start making a lot of mistakes. Don't blow his confidence in you or in himself. Take things one step at a time, building one skill at a time, rewarding him often and giving him breaks as needed. Also, remember to give him time off during the week to play in the field and/or to take trail rides with you to keep both of you fresh and interested in your work. An overworked horse is a "ring sour" horse. An overworked rider gets frustrated easily and makes mistakes that can cause injury and ruin a horse's training.

What about distractions in his surroundings and working around other horses? If he needs to be worked alone for a while, until you are both working better as a team, fine. Add work with other horses gradually and expect him to need to be reminded at first to pay attention to you exclusively. Horses are herd animals, and their natural instinct to react the way another horse reacts is hard to overcome. Be patient and be consistent. Don't be afraid to go back to working alone, for a while, if you have to. When you start working around other horses, pick those that pay attention to their riders, so your horse won't have an excuse to imitate another horse's blow up. If you must work in strange surroudings for the first time, try to have another horse and rider with you who can be an example of steadiness for your horse. If the other horse is calm, yours will probably react more calmly as well. However, don't let your horse get so attached to the companionship of one special buddy that he throws a fit if you make him go out and work alone. Trailering can be made easier with the same "buddy system" idea. Often a steadier, more experienced horse will help a younger or less experienced horse calm down during a trailer ride. Even a horse who has become a problem in a certain area or who has been spoiled or abused in a particular way can learn to overcome the problem with a patient, consistent, and persistent rider and a steady, better behaving horse buddy. Maybe he's afraid to step over a log or trotting pole. Maybe he's afraid to step through a gate because he had been hit in the side by a gate at one time. Maybe someone had used a whip on him too harshly. Use your horseman's eye to perceive the problem. Plan to adjust your horse gradually to the habit of a new behavior. Work consistently to achieve your goal. Then, your horse's attitude, his mental health, will be one of calm confidence and happy willingness to do his work. When both of you are ready to perform, physically and mentally, you are ready to begin the next step, **chapter 4, Developing the Horse and Rider Team at the Walk.**

DEVELOPING THE HORSE AND RIDER TEAM AT THE WALK

So far, you have made a lot of important decisions in planning for your show ring activities. Now, it is time to begin training yourself and your horse as a team. After all of the patient work you did in chapters 1, 2, and 3, analyzing and asking questions, you may be eager to plunge into action and start practicing your complete show ring routine immediately at walk, trot, and canter. Friends and family may be coaxing you to start showing your horse right away, so they can cheer you on from the sidelines. All of this encouragement and attention may be great for your ego, but remember these important words: patience, perception, planning, and persistence. If these words were important as you worked through chapters 1, 2, and 3, they become even more vital when you begin work under saddle. You must patiently take one step at a time, developing the perception of your "horseman's eye" and "rider's feel" for your horse. You must use these perceptions of your horse and yourself to help plan your training sessions. With care and persistence, you must be willing to work through each necessary procedure. Then, the final result will be a horse and rider team you can truly be proud of, one that is ready to compete at its best. Ready for another old saying? (Oh, boy!) "Haste makes waste." Don't rush things now, not when you've done so much the right way already.

Of course, you aren't perfect. Sometimes you can't help the urge to scrap all this planned work and just get out there and compete, especially if you hit a snag and run into a problem you can't solve. Impatience, discouragement, even frustration affect Olympic contenders at times too. After a particularly tough training session, if you feel negative thoughts creeping into your mind, take a break and seek out the advice of a knowledgeable friend or relative to give you some encouragement and an objective assessment of your progress so far. That way, you can get your mind and your energy back on track, working toward the goals you know you can achieve and enjoying your efforts as well.

All right, so how do you finally get the "show on the road"? First, you must know how to work with your horse on the lunge line. You can not only take the edge off a "fresh" horse by letting him get his energy or "play" out on a lunge line, but you can teach a horse many things on a lunge line as well, commands and ways of moving that will improve your horse's work under saddle.

HOW DOES PROPER WORK ON THE LUNGE LINE DEVELOP THE HORSE AND PREPARE HIM FOR WORK UNDER SADDLE?

In order to answer this question, you need first to understand what "proper" work on the lunge line means. Work on the line does not mean allowing the horse to race around you in a circle, with the lunge line dragging on the ground, while you snap the lunge whip wildly as you whoop at the horse to make him go faster or while you yank on his head repeatedly to slow him down. Lunge line work that really teaches the horse something has its own set of practical rules. These involve the equipment to use and how to use it effectively.

What equipment do you need? The list is basic: a sturdy halter for the horse, one that will not slip around on his head while you lunge him; a lunge line of at least 25 feet, with a chain and a snap on the horse's end; a set of side reins with adjustable elastic "give" to them; and a lunge whip of a weight and length that you can handle without strain. You can use a specialized lungeing cavesson* on the horse, but if you can't afford one of these, you can make do with a good halter that fits the horse.

As you progress in your work and lunge the horse with bridle and saddle, you may still want to have a halter on under the bridle. That way, you can attach the lunge line to the halter instead of the bridle's bit and not pull the bit sideways in the horse's mouth from the weight of the lunge line or from the horse pulling on the line. This is especially important when side reins are attached. (More about side reins and variations of them a little later here.)

A different arrangement that will allow you to attach the lunge line directly to the bridle is to run the line through the near side or inside ring of the bit on the bridle, run the line up and over the top of the horse's head behind his ears, and finally snap the line to the ring of the bit on the off side of the horse, that is the outside of what will be your circle. Then, when you change the direction of your circle from going clockwise to going counterclockwise, you will need to stop the horse, change the line around to the other side, and start the horse again. With this arrangement, be careful not to let the chain end of the line slap the horse in the eye as he moves around you in a circle. Also, remember that the pole or top of a horse's head behind his ears is a very sensitive place and that some horses are very touchy about any line or pressure being applied to this area. A horse may also be lunged in a halter with the chain end of the line run under his chin like a curb chain on a bit or over his nose and wrapped once around the noseband of the halter to prevent slipping, depending on the horse and what he will tolerate. Both the area under the chin and the area over the nose can also be very sensitive. Some horses like one arrangement better than another. Thus, when working with the halter and not the halter/bridle combination, you will need to determine which arrangement gives you control of and response from the horse without making him "freak out" in overreaction to pressure on the line. Some trainers even find that a particularly sensitive horse who is very light to handle may be able to be lunged with a lunge line that has no chain at all but is, instead, all fabric (nylon or cotton). Some people like the handler's end of the lunge line to have a safety donut which stops the line from running completely through the trainer's hands, should the horse pull on it. Other people find that the donut gets in the way of handling the line.

Instead of lungeing a horse with the saddle on, some trainers use a surcingle, which is a band that is placed around the horse's barrel just behind the withers. The band buckles up and adjusts like the girth on a saddle, except that the band has a series of rings in different places, rings where side reins can be attached to help the horse balance himself in a higher or lower frame. (More about this a little later.) While this piece of equipment is surely handy, if you can't afford one, you can improvise by attaching side reins higher up or lower down on the saddle to get the same effect that the rings on the surcingle will give you.

Some trainers also use a modified kind of running martingale*, which is known as a "training fork" and which attaches to the center of the girth at the horse's belly and comes up between the horse's front legs in two "forks" which provide rings to pass the bridle reins through. Some trainers may use extra long (six feet) reins rigged to run from the bit to behind the cantle of the saddle. Each of these pieces of equipment has its advantages and its disadvantages, which will be discussed a little further on in this chapter. Basic side reins can provide you with the training aid you may need on the lunge line, so there is no need to go running out and spending extra money buying all types of similar equipment, when you are on a limited budget.

If you are trying to decide what you would like to spend some extra money on, spend a little time first leafing through catalogs of horse equipment and talking to tack shop owners and other horsemen. Watch other horses work in the equipment. Listen. Learn. Don't just try anything on your horse. Before you run out and buy something you think you must have just because somebody else thinks it's a miracle-working device, remember this. Simple equipment with good horsemanship makes a better horse than all of the fancy gimmicks in the world in the hands of the ignorant and uneducated handler. Besides, there is no such thing as a piece of equipment that instantly "fixes" a horse with a problem. If you want him to go a certain way, you have to spend the time and effort training him, educating his mind and developing his body. A quick fix is just that. It wears off real fast and can get you into more trouble than you bargained for later.

So much for equipment. Now, how do you get started using it?

HOW DOES THE RIDER USE THE LUNGE LINE, WHIP, AND ADDITIONAL EQUIPMENT, AND WHERE AND WHEN SHOULD HE USE THEM?

Since you need a work area where your horse will pay attention and where he will have safe footing, let's look at the "where," then the "when," and last the "how." A fenced in arena with soft, safe footing is the best choice. If your horse is easily distracted or new to lungeing, work with him alone in a smaller area, like a round pen, and graduate to a full-sized (like the standard 60-foot by 100-foot rectangle) arena, when he gets the hang of things a little better. Start indoors and graduate to outdoors, where there are more distractions.

If you have neither a round pen nor an indoor arena, once again, you have to make do. Perhaps you can block off a 40-foot square of your outdoor arena and then move to using the whole arena, when your horse is better at lungeing. Whatever you do, don't try to teach a horse new to lungeing in an area where he can run away on the line, dragging you after him. Very dangerous for both of you! Make sure he isn't thinking about chasing after his buddies who are turned out in the field next to you, instead of paying attention to you. Make sure no one else is riding in your lungeing area while you get your horse used to the basic commands. You will be inviting a king size traffic accident!

Once a horse learns to lunge properly, he can be worked on the line with other responsible horsemen working around the outside edge of his circle, and he'll still pay attention to his handler standing in the center of the circle. He won't pin his ears at the other horses or charge or kick at them. He won't try to run off with you waving bodily behind him, like a tangled bed sheet on a laundry line in a summer storm.

Once you have decided on the "where," you are ready for the "when." When do you lunge the horse in your training program? First, if he is fresh and full of play, you can lunge him to get the edge off. This is done usually with just a halter, line, and whip, letting the horse play for about fifteen or twenty minutes, walking for five, trotting for five, cantering for five, and walking again for the last five. Both his mind and body will have a chance to get ready for work this way. If the horse has not had a chance to be turned out in a pasture for a few days to play, he will be fresh, so give him a chance to be a little playful, before you ask for serious work on the lunge line or under saddle. You may even find that he has less of a tendency to buck or act up under saddle with this plan of action.

Second, whenever you plan to teach a horse something new under saddle, teach the basic concept first on the lunge line, so that he doesn't have to worry about both his balance and yours, while he's learning something totally new. He can concentrate on how something feels to him alone. Besides, you will be able to watch how he moves and reacts and prepare yourself for how you can correct and help him further under saddle.

Third, you can use lunge line exercises to be described in this chapter as a way of reviewing things he already knows and as a way of warming him up for serious work under saddle, both in body and mind, whether at home or at a horse show. You can remind him of how he is to carry himself. You can improve his transitions from one gait to another. You can focus him into a certain rhythm and stride. You can work on everything from asking him to use his hindquarters and moving into the bit, to stops, to collection, to extension, to lateral bending, to work over ground poles and cavalletti and low fences. You can even work on leg yielding and sidepassing. But wait! Let's not get ahead of ourselves. What about the "how"?

Lungeing a horse properly takes thought and care, like anything else that is done right. Getting the horse to accept the equipment and handling the equipment safely come first. One of the biggest and most common problems is fear of the whip, usually a result of some bad experience with a bad handler. If your horse if terrified of whips for some reason, desensitize him to it.

Show it to him in a non-threatening way. Lay it on the ground and let him sniff it, or stand it up against a wall and lead him up to it, talking gently to him. Approach him with the whip in you hand, while a helper holds him. Make sure the whip in pointing at the ground and that you move slowly. Watch for your horse's reaction. If he looks scared or like he is about to bolt away, stop still. Let him sniff the whip again by having the helper bring him to the whip, not by moving that threatening whip closer to him while he is scared. Keep the whip still, as he builds up the courage to touch it with his nose. Encourage him softly.

Then, gradually, starting with the front leg nearest you and standing safely at his shoulder, while a helper holds his lead line and stands at his head and a little off to the other side of him, touch him softly with the shaft of the whip on his hoof. He will probably shudder and dance sideways away from you. Stop. Don't move the whip. Talk to him softly. Let him get used to it. Progress gradually like this until he will let you touch him along his shoulder and his back and ribs, along his hindquarter, and finally, down his hind leg. Don't tickle his tummy or the inside of his hind leg. He might kick out. When he's happy on one side, do the same thing on the other side of him. This whole procedure could take five or fifteen minutes or several fifteen-minute sessions over the course of several days. If one touch is all he can handle the first time out, fine. Quit there, put him in his stall, and try again in a couple of hours or even the next day. Soon, he won't be afraid of the whip, and you will be able to raise and lower it slowly near him, without having him go ballistic on you.

The next problem is the lunge line. If he is afraid of the touch of the line, use the same kind of desensitizing procedure as you did with the whip, touching him with the line and gradually draping it over his back and touching his sides and the outsides of his legs with it. Be careful not to get him tangled in it, or he will panic and all of your patient work will be set back to square one. Experiment with how he is most comfortable with the line and the chain, as described earlier. Remember, at this stage, you are using only the halter, lunge line, and whip. Once he is happy with the equipment, you are ready for some action. Finally! Okay, okay! Better safe than sorry, right?

Begin with the lunge line attached to the horse's halter. Stand at his shoulder and let about three feet of line hang between you and him. Take the rest of the line and lay it in big loops, one on top of the other into the palm of one hand, so that the loops will uncoil easily. Do not wrap the line around your hand. If the horse bolts, you will be tangled in it. Which hand should you loop the line into? If the horse is going to be moving around you clockwise, loop the excess line into your left hand, as you face the horse at his right shoulder. The reverse is true, when the horse will be going counterclockwise.

Next pick up the handle of the lunge whip in the same hand that is holding the excess line, so that the handle does not interfere with the loops of line. (Make sure the whip is pointed at the ground at your side.) If the whip and line appear to be a bulky mess to hold in one hand, try making the loops larger, so that there are fewer of them and thus less of the line in the palm of your hand. Your free hand will be used on the line between your body and the horse's head, with the same gentle feel that you would take on a bridle rein, using your fingers, little finger toward the horse, knuckles up, almost like you were playing piano keys.

Let's say that you first want to teach the horse to lunge a circle to the left around you. The key idea with lungeing is to start small and then get bigger. Why? If your body is closer to the horse when he is supposed to be paying attention to something new, he is more likely to keep his focus on you. As soon as he gets the idea, you can give him more space. It works like this.

Stand at his shoulder, left hand on the line for cueing between your body and the horse's halter, right hand at your side holding the whip handle and the excess line. Move your left hand out to the left side of you at the level of the horse's mouth, raise the whip gently to touch him on his left hip, and say, "Walk" or "Walk on." He should begin to take a few steps to begin that left circle. Turn to face his shoulder as he moves on and feed him a little more line, maybe from three to six feet. Keep the whip pointed at him at the level of his hip.

If he walks off quietly, he may still turn around and wonder why you aren't coming along. He may think that you were going to lead him. The idea is to send him away from you. If he comes back in, start over again. Don't get in front of him, and don't back up to make up for his mistakes. Insist that he walk that circle, while you stay in the middle of the circle and merely turn to keep facing his shoulder. If he finally gets the idea, praise him. Once he has the idea on a ten-foot circle, you can gradually feed him more line and encourage him to make the circle larger by pointing at his hip with the whip and repeating the verbal command. The two of you should look like the photo.

Correct position and use of equipment to begin working horse correctly on a lunge line.

Don't make the mistake of losing contact on that line by feeding him too much line at one time and letting the line droop into the arena dirt. You will lose his attention, because you have lost contact with his front end. Keep his attention by keeping the light, elastic feel of the line, by keeping eye contact with him, and by keeping the whip raised and pointed at him at the level of his hip.

Now that he's out there walking a circle, he may quickly get the idea that he can move more freely and get a little excited. Maybe he begins to trot or even canter. But wait! This chapter is supposed to be about developing you and your horse at the walk. What do you do now? First, don't panic, and second, don't get angry.

Lower the whip to a neutral position at your side and begin half-halting him on the line. What's a half-halt? Simple. Each time you see his inside hind leg coming forward, squeeze the line in your left hand to resist his forward motion for one beat (or step he takes) like you were squeezing a rubber ball in your fingers. Keep your hand low and don't lose the original elastic feel of the line, after you release the squeeze. Talk to him calmly. Say:

"Easy. Walk. Walk." Always use the same tone of voice for the walk command. Eventually he'll get the idea. When he does, praise him. If he starts trotting or cantering again, repeat the above procedure.

Don't expect him to develop consistency in ten minutes. This whole thing could take days to teach, with about fifteen minutes spent at a time. Be patient, be perceptive of his reactions and your corrections, and be persistent. If you need a helper on the sidelines to observe the two of you and to tell you if you asked him too soon or too late or too harshly or not firmly enough, fine. Maybe you have to get the hang of this lungeing thing too, so don't expect him to be a genius. If someone else can actually show you this exact procedure, watch first, and then try it. Remember the part about coordinating your squeeze with the inside hind leg. It will become very important as your work with him proceeds. Remember also that the line influences his front end, while the whip influences his hindquarters.

Last, remember, not to try this on a horse who is so fresh that he needs to be turned out in the pasture first to blow off some steam. If you want to teach him something new, you have to get his attention, not have him dragging you all over the place or walking over top of you. He's like a kindergarten child. If he needs to play, he'll never get the lesson. Of course, if he already knows how to lunge basically, you are already one step farther ahead of the game and you need only work on coordinating your own aids and developing your horseman's eye in reading his reactions to your commands.

Fine so far. You have him walking a circle around you. So? Before you can achieve anything else, that walk needs to be long, low, relaxed, and consistent. While that picture may sound simple to create, it will take focus on your part and his to get that picture and to maintain that walk consistently. If he starts to drag along, take one step toward his hindquarters and touch him lightly with your whip, if you have to, as you repeat the verbal command, "Walk." If he rushes ahead, use half-halts to steady his pace and lower your whip to a more neutral position. If his head is high, lower the hand you have on the line and use very, very light half-halts once every stride or once every other stride, just as the inside hind leg is coming forward. At the same time you half-halt, encourage him very lightly with the whip. You will find that he begins to lengthen his stride, stretch out his neck, and — You got it! — lower his head to the level of his withers. His nose will probably stick out, and the front of his face won't be on a perfectly vertical plane, but that's okay for now.

At this stage, you have achieved the walk you need as a starting place for all other developments at the walk. Like a dancer or a runner who does stretching exercises before he begins his routine, this walk will serve to limber up and relax your horse's body and mind. While he is walking, practice asking him to shorten his stride for one circle and then practice asking him to lengthen his stride again for another circle. To shorten, use half-halts. To lengthen use very, very light half-halts with your line hand held very low and use the whip cue very lightly. He will soon get the idea that there are different types of walking. This is the beginning of the lenghtening and collection you will develop more with side reins and ultimately later under saddle. (Remember, lengthening means a longer stride or frame, and shortening means a shorter, rounder stride or frame. Both kinds of strides have the same rhythm, but different size steps, larger versus smaller. Speeding up is not lengthening. Slowing down is not shortening.) Now you see how important it is for the horse to get his balance without a rider and figure out his rhythm and his frame (with your kind help, of course). Be sure to practice these exercises in both directions and not to work on them for more than ten or fifteen minutes. Be sure also that the horse is using his hind quarters as he moves, reaching well under himself with each step. Point the whip at his hindquarters to keep giving him the idea that he should keep using himself back there.

After he has been walking for a while, you can begin to teach the halt on the line. Don't try this while he is still eager to move about. Wait until the last five minutes of the workout. He'll be more willing to stop and stand quietly. First, lower your whip to your side, a neutral position. Then, half-halt on the line a little more strongly and say in a low-pitched voice, "Ho!" or "Whoa!" He may hesitate for a moment and continue to walk. Keep repeating the command calmly, half-halt with voice command, until he gets the idea. Let him stand for ten or fifteen seconds, once he stops, but don't lose eye contact with him and don't let the line drag on the ground. When he gets the idea that he should halt until you give the next command, send him off again at the walk.

Repeat this exercise a few times, stopping him for a different number of seconds each time, so he doesn't think that he will stop only for a few seconds or that every time he stops he's going to come in to you and stop working altogether.

Once he has halted quietly, you may use gentle tugs on the line and the command, "Come," to ask him to walk to you, or you may say, "Ho," or "Whoa" to keep him standing and walk out to him instead. The choice is yours. Don't be concerned that he hasn't halted with all four feet squarely under him yet. Let him become familiar with one idea at a time. Remember, you are teaching all of these basic commands with only a halter and lunge line and lunge whip.

Only after the above has been accomplished can you begin to put the pieces together and start to ask for smooth, attentive transitions from walk to halt and from halt back to walk again. Now, you can start expecting him to halt more squarely, but if he is still a little spread out, don't worry. Once he graduates to work on the side reins, you can put the polish on his halt. For now, be happy that he responds crisply but quietly and keeps his mind on his work. Imagine what a help this preliminary lunge line work will be in keeping his attention, once you are on his back, teaching the same concepts under saddle! So, now comes the next question.

HOW DO EXERCISES ON THE LUNGE LINE WITH GROUND POLES AND CAVALLETTI* DEVELOP THE HORSE PHYSICALLY AND MENTALLY AND HELP THE HORSE PREPARE FOR WORK UNDER SADDLE?

Before beginning work with the saddle, bridle, and some form of side reins, you need to work through one more series of simple exercises, with ground poles and cavalletti. If your horse is not used to stepping over a ground pole, you will have to desensitize him the way you did with the lunge whip.

First, lay a pole on the ground in your arena. Before you attempt to work your horse over the pole on the lunge line, simply walk him up to the pole calmly and lead him over it. Practice doing this in both directions. If he hesitates, just step over it first and more than likely he will follow you, because he trusts you. Don't get in front of him, though. Stay at his side, because he may decide to jump over it the first few times. You don't want him landing on top of you. If he outright refuses, lead him on his left, use your lunge whip in your left hand, with your right hand on the lead line. Gently reach behind you to touch the hocks or below on his left hind leg with the whip. You still have to keep facing forward, calmly walking over the pole. Most of the time, a little touch with the whip will encourage him to take that first scary step, but your body language must smoothly and calmly encourage him forward, or he will simply shy sideways away from the whip instead of going forward.

Another trick is to place the pole perpendicular to a wall or the rail of the arena. Then, as you lead him, he has no choice but to go forward or backward, because the wall or rail on the right side stops him from going sideways to the right, and your presence stops him from going sideways to the left and avoiding the task of stepping over the pole. To practice going the other direction, you have to lead him on the right and place the pole so that it is perpendicular to a wall or rail on his left.

If he still refuses, ask a helper to use the lunge whip and gently tap him on his hind legs, as you lead him over the pole. Make sure the helper stays opposite his shoulder, or the helper may get kicked by an overreacting horse. Which side should the helper stand on? If the horse wants to shy to the right, let the helper stand on the right. If the horse wants to shy to the left, let the helper stand on the left. If the horse backs up, go with him until he stops. If you are gentle, he'll probably only take a step or two anyway. Don't overreact in punishing him. He tends to back away from something that he is afraid of. Lead him up to the pole again. Give him a little more time to figure it out. Encourage him. Tell him it's all right. You may have to go through the same desentisizing exercise with a cavalletti, before you actually begin work with cavalletti on the lunge line. These preliminaries take a little time, to be sure, but you will find that they save a lot of frustration later on down the road, when you want to get some important exercise accomplished.

Once the horse will accept stepping over ground poles and cavalletti individually, you are ready to get down to some constructive work. Start with two ground poles and graduate up to four over several lessons, with each lesson being ten or fifteen minutes. Lay them on the ground in the arc of the circle your horse will take as he walks around you on the lunge line. Before you attempt to lunge him over any new setup, lead him over them in both directions a few times first to familiarize him with them. At the walk, the poles should be about two and a half to three feet apart, depending on the length of your horse's stride and whether you are working on his natural walk, on extending his walk, or on collecting his walk. The poles should be a little closer together at the inside of the arc and a little farther apart at the outside of the arc, like the spokes of a wheel, like this:

Your horse travels this arc as he circles you.————>

This is your position————————>X

Start with two poles spaced to accommodate your horse's natural stride. Ask him to walk over them several times in each direction with a business-like walk and without hitting any poles with his hooves. Then, move them about six inches closer together. Lead him over the new arrangement. Then, lunge him over them. Surprise! He takes smaller steps, doesn't he, so he doesn't hit the poles with his hooves? If he hits the poles on the first try, see if they need adjusted or if you need to half-halt him a little to help him get the idea. Soon he will figure out that he can keep the same rhythm but round himself up and take smaller steps. This is the beginning of collection.

How do you get him to do this business-like walk going over the poles? Pay attention to these details. His head should be at the level of his withers or even a little lower. He should be paying attention to what he is doing. If he is not, vibrate the lunge line gently with your finger tips, like you are playing a violin string, so he feels the little signals and keeps his focus on his job. You will be able to use this gentle but subtle technique later with the reins while you are in the saddle to keep his attention from wandering.

His stride should be smooth and relaxed. It is your responsibility to aim him straight at the center of those poles. Stay opposite his shoulder. Don't let him come at those poles from an odd angle, or he will be sure to hit them as he tries to walk over. Point the whip at his shoulder, if he tries to avoid the poles by stepping toward the inside of the circle with his front end. This action drives him back out onto the correct circle. If he wants to turn to the outside of the circle to avoid having to work over the poles, his nose will start to tip to the outside and his hip will turn inside. Keep his attention and that light, elastic contact on the line as he goes forward. Use half-halts on the line to keep his nose from pointing outside and point the whip at his hip to keep him from dropping his hip too far to the inside.

Keep him looking at and focused on his job. If he wants to slow down too much, keep him walking forward with your whip raised to the level of and pointed at his hip. Use the lunge line correctly. Vibrate it occasionally. If you droop the line in the dirt and let him wander into the poles, you will get a sloppy performance. You want a crisp, business-like job here, so focus yourself on him and expect to get the best. You are both worth the effort. Stop and praise him when he has done well.

You can work him over up to four poles this way, but don't overdo it. Work on this exercise for only about ten minutes at a time, after you have worked him on his other walking exercises. This is demanding work for your horse, physically and mentally, because it is so precise and he must really concentrate.

Next, you can move the poles about six inches farther apart and begin to work on extending the length of his stride. Keep the same procedure and the same rhythm. Lead him over; lunge him over. Make sure he's relaxed and paying attention. Praise him when he does it right. If he is confused, don't try to get him to collect and extend all on the same day. Give him time to adjust. Taking that little extra time, paying attention and reading your horse's needs, you will find that more advanced exercises later come a lot easier. Both of you will be a confident, prepared team.

Okay! Now it's time to try some work with cavalletti. After that, it will be time to add the side reins and, finally, to begin work under saddle. You're making definite progress. Don't let anybody rush you. If you need it, seek only the advice of people who know what they are talking about. Your friends may want you to rush headlong into advanced work, but be smart enough to lay this good foundation patiently. It will pay off in big dividends later.

Use the same exercises and procedures with the cavalletti that you did with the ground poles. So, what's the big difference? Why not just stick with ground poles and not bother with cavalletti at all? Cavalletti have a special advantage. If you use cavalletti set at a height of six to eight inches off the ground, your horse will really have to watch his feet and work harder physically and mentally to get the job done right. This work builds his muscles and his mind. It is very demanding, so don't overdo it. Be sure to praise your horse when he does well. Work only five minutes each direction over cavalletti AFTER you have warmed him up on flat exercises for ten minutes. You will be surprised to see how much more polish and consistency these exercises add to his stride.

After he is happy and consistent working the walk over both ground poles and cavalletti, then you can add the side reins as an aid to helping him collect his frame and balance himself even better. This must be done VERY carefully, however, to avoid cramping his muscles and ruining his pleasant attitude about his work.

First, tack him up as if you were ready to ride him, with the halter on under the bridle, so you can attach the lunge line to the halter and the side reins to the bit on the bridle. If you are using a hunt seat saddle, run the stirrups up the leathers and secure them from bumping around or remove them altogether. The stirrups on a Western saddle don't usually move around so much, because they are stabilized by the fenders, but you can tie them to the girth with little pieces of bailing twine, if you need to. Just remember to untie them when you are ready to mount your horse. Remove the regular reins from the bridle, but don't attach the side reins to the bridle yet. If you are using a lungeing surcingle, you will not even need any saddle, because the rings on the surcingle will provide you with a place to secure the other ends of the side reins, that is the ends not attached to the bridle's bit. (More on exactly how to adjust side reins a little later on here.)

Have you ever watched a dancer or an athlete warm up for practice or competition? What does he or she do? He/she stretches his/her muscles gently before he/she begins work that will command the muscles to contract. Otherwise, the muscles would cramp up. The same is true for the horse. His body must be relaxed and stretched out, before you ask him to collect his frame and perform any specialized movements. Thus, it is very, very important that you work your horse on the lunge line WITHOUT SIDE REINS for fifteen minutes (seven to eight minutes in each direction) as a warm-up for his muscles. This strategy will also help him to focus his attention and get his mind ready to concentrate fully on the more difficult work to come once the side reins are attached. Okay, then, here is the next logical question.

HOW ARE THE SIDE REINS ADJUSTED AND USED CORRECTLY?

After the warm-up, you will adjust the side reins for the type of frame or shape you want to teach your horse to develop as he moves. You must be very careful to adjust the side reins correctly, or all of your patient work on your horse's stride, balance, and attitude will be ruined. Side reins adjusted too tight make for many problems:

1. a horse who suffers with cramped back, shoulder, and hindquarter muscles;

2. a horse who **either** gets behind the bit ("over bent") to avoid excess pressure on his mouth and to relieve muscle cramps **or** who "lays" on the bit and lets his mouth go numb from the pressure so he can stretch his neck a little and relieve his cramped neck, shoulder, and back muscles;

3.   a horse whose stride is shortened artificially so much that his hind legs lose their power and natural spring ("impulsion"), causing his stride to become droopy and heavy on his forehand. His walk becomes doggy, his trot steps have no definition, and his canter falls apart from a true three-beat to a sloppy four-beat, as he "canters in front and trots behind."

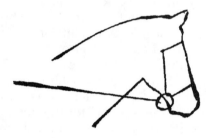

Ahead of the Bit (Stretched Out)

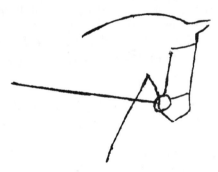

On the Bit (Face on Vertical)

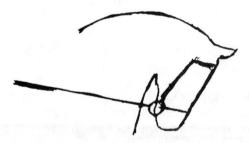

Behind the Bit (Overbent, Face Behind Vertical)

Quite a potential disaster, isn't it? Look at the diagram to see what to look for in how your horse carries his head.

Okay, so how should the side reins be adjusted and which type should you use? Remember, we mentioned that there would be several ways of fitting your horse with side reins? Remember also that back in chapter 2 you analyzed your horse's conformation. Take a close look again at how your horse naturally carries his head and neck in relation to the rest of his body and go back and review what you plan to do with him. If his neck comes out of his body at a high angle, he carries his head naturally higher, a conformation trait suited more to English events. If your horse's neck comes out of his body at a more level (flat) angle, he carries his head lower and is more suited to Western events. This is true even when he is walking relaxed and stretched out. When he is relaxed and his stride is long, you should also notice that his nose tends to poke out a little in front of him and his face is not on a vertical plain. When he collects himself, his whole body rounds, like a Slinky toy rounded together. He may be rounded in a higher arc if his head and neck are higher or in a lower arc, if his head and neck are lower. The front of his face, though, will be on a more vertical plain when he is collected than it is when he is stretched out. So?

WHAT DO ALL OF THESE REMINDERS ABOUT YOUR HORSE'S CONFORMATION AND MOVEMENT HAVE TO DO WITH ADJUSTING SIDE REINS?

Plenty. Certain types of side rein setups are better for Western schooling and certain ones are better for English (hunt seat) schooling.

Let's start with the horse whose conformation and way of going are best suited to Western events. His side reins should be adjusted so that he can carry his head level with his withers, with his body in a long, low frame, and with the front of his face almost on the vertical plain or with his nose poked out just a tad. He should be able to keep this picture at any gait. The side reins should help him but not force his face behind that vertical plain just to keep his head low and his stride slow. Forcing him means the side reins are too tight, making for all of the problems mentioned above.

For Western schooling, side reins can be adjusted in several ways, with just enough tension to keep a constant, light, elastic touch on the horse's mouth through the bit. The horse should step fluidly in a natural way from behind into the bit, striding his back hooves into the imprints his front hooves leave in the dirt. He should flex his neck at the pole of his head and relax his jaw to balance lightly on the bit with the energy that comes forward from his hindquarters. Here are the possible setups.

1.   Tie the stirrups to the girth to stabilize them and tie the free ends of the side reins to the stirrups, making sure both side reins are even in length and height.

2.   Use a "training fork," a kind of running martingale, which is attached to the center of the girth, then splits into two forks, which come up between the horse's front legs. Each fork has a loop to run the side reins through. The free ends of the side reins can then be tied together and attached to the stirrups, looped behind the cantle, or looped behind the swell of the saddle, depending on the shape of the frame you wish the horse to establish.

Whatever you decide to do, caution is the key word here. The training fork is especially tricky. With it, there may be the danger of forcing the horse's head down too low and getting him behind the bit or leaning on his forehand. The training fork, since it is so low, also makes it more difficult for the horse to transfer the idea of the feel on the reins from the side rein feel to the feel of having the rider's hands on the reins as he sits in the saddle. Here are some other cautions.

1.   Never keep side reins attached when the horse is standing still. You might encourage him to lean on the bit, a bad habit.

2.   Do not use side reins while you are riding the horse. He should be paying attention to your hands, seat, and legs, not to some artificial device.

3.   Start with the side reins a notch or two looser than you actually plan to work in as a finished result, and work the horse gradually into the proper position over several lessons to develop his muscles and avoid strain.

4.   Always work fifteen minutes without side reins before using them and use them for no more than fifteen minutes total at a time.

5. Walk your horse through all exercises on the flat, then use poles, then use cavalletti, then use the side reins. Don't just jump into the use of the side reins.

These same basic cautions apply to working your horse to prepare him for hunt seat events, but of course, the side reins will be adjusted differently than for Western events, to help your horse carry his whole frame in a shape suited to hunt seat classes. How should you proceed for hunt seat preparation?

1. Using the rings on the lungeing surcingle or the billet straps on the English saddle, attach the free ends of the side reins higher up than for Western, so that the horse's frame more closely approximates where the rider's hands and rein contact will be in the saddle. **BUT**

2. Attach the side reins at the level of the horse's shoulder, about where the rider's knee would be, and gradually change the position to be closer to the withers, as in #1 above, **especially if** the horse is particularly green or stretched out in his frame to begin with.

The lower the side reins, the lower the horse will keep his head, in general, and the lower his frame. Remember, however, the goal is not just to force the head down or to "set" the head. The expression "set the head" is a dangerous misconception. The shape of the horse's entire spine will either be in a lower or higher arc. The head will be higher because the arc is rounder and lower because the arc is lower and more shallow. You must train your horseman's eye to see the shape of the whole horse and to watch the quality of his stride, not just to look at his head. Remember, work flat exercises without side reins before exercises with side reins, and, again, the same holds true for work over poles or cavalletti.

Finally, after all of this preparation, you should be ready to mount your horse and start to work him under saddle. Great! At last, you say. But not so fast. Let's take a moment to examine your position in the saddle.

Everything you do as a rider will affect both your horse's attitude and his movement or "way of going." To get the best performance, you must move in harmony with your horse. You cannot do this if you are sitting on him incorrectly to begin with.

WHAT SHOULD YOUR POSITION IN THE SADDLE LOOK AND FEEL LIKE?

Whether you ride Western or English (hunt seat), your seat and body position must put you in harmony with the horse's center of gravity and ready to move with him, so you do not get left behind his action or fall forward ahead of his action. Your horse should be standing at a quiet halt, so you can concentrate on your position. As you settle into the saddle, sit up tall and sit down directly on your seat bones. First, you may need to stand in your stirrups and then sit straight down to feel those seat bones under you. Then, drop your stirrups and let your leg hang. Do not slouch back on your tail bone or slump forward onto your crouch. Keep your chin level and your eyes looking out ahead of you. Square your shoulders and let them hang naturally, directly over your hips. Make sure all of your joints are limber and relaxed, even your wrists, elbows, and ankles.

Let your leg hang naturally, so that your heel is right under your hip and the side of your leg is lying gently against the horse's side. Don't pick up your stirrups yet. Concentrate on feeling an even, smooth contact from your seat and crotch area down through the inside of your thighs and the inside of your calf muscles. Your knees should neither pinch tight nor pop out away from the horse. Your position must be correct now, or you will give your horse the wrong signals in every movement the two of you try together.

If your knee pinches, you are probably sitting too much on your crotch and front of your thighs and not enough on your seat bones. Correct your seat by spreading your legs and making sure you are on your seat bones. Then, the knee problem will be easier to fix. If you have to, put both hands on the front of the saddle, have a friend stand at your horse's head to steady him, and lift one leg at a time slowly, knee to your chest, like you are pumping a bicycle. Make sure you still sit up straight. This simple exercise will spread your legs and make it easier to sit on your seat bones when you put your leg back down.

What if the knee pops out? Then, you are probably gripping with the back of your calf muscles and your heels. Read on to see how to fix this. If your heels are digging into the horse and you are gripping the horse with the back of your calf muscles, reach around, to one leg at a time, to the back of your thigh, midway between your crotch and your knee with the hand on that side of your body. Just lift and roll your relaxed leg so that your crotch widens and the muscles on the inside of your thigh can stretch, grow longer, and lie against the horse. Then, surprise! It will be much easier for you to place the side of your calf against the horse and to stop gripping with your heels.

One major word of caution: **Don't try to fix leg position problems working from your heel up. Start with the source of the problem, the seat. Everything starts from your seat.** If you are slouching, work from the seat up to correct your position in the shoulders and upper body. Then, work down from the seat as described above. If your leg or heel is the problem, work from the seat down, letting your leg grow long and keeping an alignment of shoulder, hip, and heel. Don't expect to attain the ideal position in one second either. Maybe you have been sitting incorrectly for a long time. Okay, so now you have to retrain your muscles just like you are helping your horse develop his muscles. Be patient with yourself and keep working on yourself. Persistence and intelligent effort pay off in time.

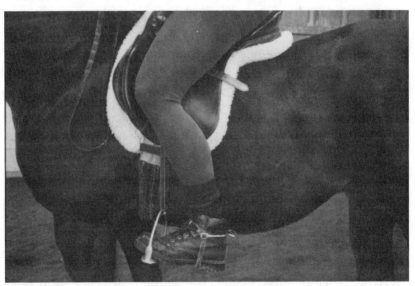

Example of correct seat and leg position in the saddle.

Believe it or not, the type of saddle you are using can also affect your ability to attain the correct seat and body position. Watch out for these potential problems. If you have a hunt seat saddle built exclusively for jumping, you may have problems sitting correctly when you work on the flat. Why? The tree of a jumping saddle is tilted forward, to help you move with the horse over fences. When you sit down, however, you end up in a "chair seat," with your seat behind the horse's action and your legs out in front of you. Without realizing why, or even that you are doing it, you may find yourself trying to "catch up" to the horse's movement by slumping your shoulders forward, hollowing your back, sitting on your crotch, and pinching your knees to keep your balance. If you can't correct a bad position in the saddle you have, the saddle may be the problem, not you. Hunt seat work is done best in an all-purpose saddle, one built to allow you to sit in balance with the horse during flat work as well as over fences. Try to avoid working in a saddle made exclusively for jumping at this stage of your riding career.

What about Western saddles? Check the seat of the saddle out before you mount up. A roping saddle has the seat built up higher in front just behind the swell and horn and lower in back by the cantle. This construction allows the roper to stand in his stirrups to balance into the front of his saddle with his crotch and upper thigh for support during roping. A roping saddle, however, is a disadvantage for a Western Pleasure rider who needs a more level seat that allows him to balance in the center of the horse's action, because once the roper sits down, he feels his seat pushed back against the cantle. The Western Pleasure rider should look for a level seat.

The way the stirrups are hung from the tree on a Western saddle can also pose a problem. Ideally, when you sit in the saddle, you should be able to keep your hip aligned right over your heel. The stirrups should be right next to your feet, ready to be picked up by your toes. You should not have to slide your legs forward or backward to find the stirrups. If you do, the fenders and stirrups have been hung from the saddle tree in a style uncomfortable for you and you will never feel comfortable and in harmony with your horse's movement.

Width of the saddle tree is another consideration for both the hunt seat and Western rider. When you sit down in the saddle, the tree may be set too wide or too narrow for you, even if it seems to fit your horse's back. The saddle must be comfortable for both of you. If your inner thighs are screaming, "I can't take this! I feel like I'm doing a split!" the tree is too wide. If you feel like you are sitting on a narrow board that is ready to cut you in half, the tree is too narrow. Find a saddle that you and your horse can work in comfortable, and you will be more assured of working in harmony with your horse.

Fine, so now you are sitting at the halt in harmony with your horse. What's next? Pick up the stirrups. For Western, you should simply raise your toes to find the stirrups and slide your feet in up to the ball of the foot. You should feel an even pressure along the bottom of your foot from the big bone behind your big toe to the bones behind your little toe. If you can't get that even feel, don't force it. Let your legs grow longer from the seat down the inside of your legs to your heels, and your muscles will gradually stretch to let your feet settle evenly in the stirrups. Let your heels sink lower than your toes in the same way. Don't force your heels down or push on your stirrups so that your feet and lower legs shoot out in front of you. Remember that shoulder, hip, heel vertical alignment.

When you pick up your stirrups in a hunt seat saddle, achieve the same feel, except that your stirrups will be a notch or two shorter and your knees a little more bent. If your stirrups have been set for jumping, lower them two holes. Flat work must allow you to ride down through your horse. If you are perched above his back like a jockey, you will never be able to use your seat, back, and legs properly to school your horse effectively. You can always raise your stirrups two holes again, when you are ready to jump.

Now it's time to pick up the reins. For schooling purposes, whether you are riding Western or hunt seat, work first with the reins in two hands. Neck reining Western will come a little later and much easier if you work two-handed first. For hunt seat, you should be using a simple snaffle bit (Egg Butt, Full Cheek, or D-Ring). For Western, a bit with a snaffle mouthpiece, short shanks, and a curb chain (such as a Tom Thumb or Argentine snaffle) will give you the advantage of both snaffle and curb action if you work correctly. Of course, you can also use a simple snaffle to school the Western horse and graduate him later to the Tom Thumb, depending on what he is already working well in. If your horse's mouth is insensitive from someone pulling on him, Western or hunt seat, it is always better to go back to a simple snaffle and re-educate his mouth to be sensitive to light touches. Putting a harsher bit into a horse's mouth to solve a hard-mouth problem (like a long-shank Western curb, a Western cathedral bit, or an English Kimberwick or Pelham) only makes the problem worse.

Using a harsher bit is sort of like yelling at a person. If all you do is yell at him, pretty soon, you have to keep yelling louder and louder to get him to do what you want. Finally, he just gets so accustomed to the yelling, that he never takes you seriously and starts ignoring you altogether. Your horse will do the same thing. Keep getting more and more harsh, and pretty soon you have a horse that will not listen no matter how hard you pull and no matter how harsh the bit is. Better to educate his mind and mouth than to destroy his attitude and his sensitive mouth tissues.

Take a rein in each hand, reins near the tips of your fingers, hands low in front of you, elbows comfortably at your sides. Hold your hands about four inches apart, just above the horse's withers, thumbs up, little fingers pointing toward your horse's head. Whether Western or hunt seat, for now take up the slack in the reins until you have a **very light, elastic feel** of the bridle. If your horse moves his jaw, his tongue, or his lips, you should feel it and follow the movement by squeezing or releasing the squeeze of your fingers on the reins very gently.

One last thought before you move your horse out at the walk: remember the **cardinal rules for schooling horse and rider.**

PATIENCE: willingness to take the time needed with yourself as the rider and with the horse and to retrace steps back to an easier level, slower speed, and more basic exercise, when problems arise.

PERCEPTION: opening your mind and tuning into your own body and your horse's responses, to develop understanding of what you and your horse need. Thus, you will be able to tell the differences between over schooling and under schooling horse and rider and will see and correct mistakes easier and sooner.

PLANNING: willingness to think of the whole horse and the whole rider and to focus on goals and the steps and time needed to achieve them.

That's a lot to think about, isn't it? Be sure to review the above thoughts whenever you run into rough spots. They will help you put your head on straight again and move forward. Okay. Let's get moving!

HOW IS THE WALK DEVELOPED UNDER SADDLE?

So far, you have already developed a steady, fluid, relaxed walk on the lunge line. You have taught your horse the beginnings of collection and extension. You have taught him to work an even circle, to halt quietly, and to walk on crisply. You have taught him to pay attention to his job, to you, and to where he places his feet. Now, you have to achieve the same goals under saddle. The lunge line work should make it easier for your horse to get the idea of what you want, because he has already practiced it on his own, without you on his back, when he was on the lunge line. He should be ready to learn to respond correctly to your cues from the saddle.

Ask him to walk forward from the halt as he stands on the rail in your arena. You can be going around to the left or to the right, whichever is easier for him at first. Horses are right-sided and left-sided just like people are right-handed or left-handed, so he will be stiffer on one side than on the other. When teaching him something new, start on his better side. Almost simultaneously, open your chest a little, scoop your seat bones a little, and squeeze your calf muscles a little to get your horse moving. Go back into neutral after you ask and ask again, if he does not respond. Reinforce your physical cues (aids) with the voice command you used while he was on the lunge line earlier. You can always drop the voice cue, after he gets a better idea of what you want. You can't give voice commands in the show ring, remember. They are not allowed.

As he takes his first step, be sure to follow his motion quietly with the reins, from your fingers all the way up into your shoulders, and to follow the motion with your seat and back. If your horse seems to be hesitating, make your feel of the reins lighter, so he doesn't think you are asking him to halt with your hands and go with your seat and legs at the same time. That would confuse him. If he is simply not paying attention, vibrate one rein a little and then the other, like you did the lunge line, to get his attention. Then, ask him to walk off. If he still doesn't move, he's daydreaming. Use one rein and turn his head gently, enough to make him take a step sideways with a front foot. Then, ask him to walk off straight ahead. He'll have to do something, because you have changed his balance by making him move one foot. Green horses often have this problem, so don't be angry with him. Keep practicing consistently. Eventually, he'll get the idea that just a touch means "pay attention and go forward."

As he walks forward, be sure that you are looking out ahead of you where you both are going. If you look down, your body will weigh on his forehand and he'll be sluggish. If you look to one side, the slight changes in your muscles and your seat bone pressure as your body unconsciously follows your eyes will make him travel crooked. Allow your hips and lower back to move with his hips. Relax and follow him.

Concentrate on feeling his motion and matching it with your body, until you both feel like one fluid motion. Your seat and legs will be controlling his hips and rear legs, and your hands will be controlling his forehand. Feel him move: left hip and hind leg into right shoulder and front leg; right hip and hind leg into left shoulder and front leg. Feel the energy from one hind leg into the opposite rein, as the motion moves through the horse from back to front. Keep the light contact on the rein but follow the motion. See if you can keep this steady, light feel and rhythm all the way around the arena. Especially down the long side, aim straight at a point distant from you, to keep your body straight and him moving on a straight line.

Corners are the tricky part. Look out ahead of you at the shape of the corner. Make it even and round. A stride or two before the corner, be especially conscious of when his inside hind leg is coming forward. (Remember, you were using his inside hind leg as a signal to cue him with a squeeze on the line and to keep the circle as he walked up into the bridle when you worked him on the lunge line.) Feel the energy come from that inside hind leg into the outside rein. Keep the outside rein steady and your outside leg steady, just behind the girth, to keep the shape of the bend. Use the moment when his inside hind leg is coming up to squeeze gently with your inside rein and to contract the calf muscle of your inside leg against his side. Then, release. On the next stride, do the same thing again. You will find that the little squeeze helps to tip his nose to follow the shape of the corner and helps him to step under himself and round his whole body to the shape of the curve. Since you asked him to tip his nose just when his legs were moving to take the shape of the corner (when the inside hind leg was coming forward) it's easy for him to carry himself and you through the corner without falling onto his shoulder or shifting his hips or any other part of him out of the shape you want. You have used the horse's own natural energy to show him how comfortable it will be for him to perform as you ask. Kind of neat, isn't it?

HOW DO YOU LENGTHEN (EXTEND) HIS STRIDE, AND HOW DO YOU SHORTEN (COLLECT) HIS STRIDE?

Coming down the long side of the arena, do more than just follow his motion. To increase the length of this stride (not make him go faster but longer) increase the motion of your hips and the action of your seat bones **for a stride or two**, while lightening up on the feel of the bridle. You will find that he keeps the same rhythm but takes bigger steps. Don't keep pushing at him with your seat. If he is sluggish, use your calf muscles with your seat for a stride or two. Then, sit quietly and follow his motion to see how many strides of big steps he will give you. Usually, a green horse will give you three or four or even five. Then, he will start to daydream and poke along. Keep his attention with your cues again. Gradually, he will be able to take not only bigger steps but keep his attention on the job longer. This is a real stretching exercise, so don't force the issue for more than a few minutes at a time at first. Make sure you stop asking for extension before you get to a corner. Otherwise, at this stage, he could get sloppy on his corners. You can work up to getting long strides all the way around the arena, corners included, like you do with every other new activity.

What if, instead, he is one of those horses who has a "big motor" and who would rather rush around the arena? You can't teach him to extend quietly, because he's too busy wanting to rush around anyway. You will have to work on circles with him first and begin to teach him to pay attention better. Then, you can teach him to extend, and he won't think you just want him to go faster and race. Work on circles first. Here's how.

Use the same cues you used to create nice round bends on the corners of the arena. To create a circle, though, just keep the bend going all the way around to a full circle. Start by making circles at the corners of the arena and then going back on the rail. If he tends to rush his corners and wants to race the long sides of the arena, circles often get his attention back and round him up enough to keep him from falling apart once he is on the rail again. Sometimes it takes more than one circle to get his attention. Don't let him come out of the circle until he is ready to give to your hands and obey your legs. He will soon get the idea that whenever he wants to race, he will be going nowhere fast in a gentle circle, about twenty feet in diameter. He'll learn to quit playing around, because he's not getting anywhere. Don't get angry and beat him or yank on his mouth. That will just upset him and make him want to go faster, away from you and your bad temper.

Circles can also be used to help him stretch and strengthen the muscles that help him carry himself on a bend. He will become much more flexible, supple, and light to the touch if you practice circles at various places in the arena for about five or six minutes in each direction at the walk each day. If you **half halt on the circle** and ask him to **collect his stride on the circle**, you will already have established a collected gait. That makes it easier for him to get the idea of collection on the rail. You already know how to half halt the lunge line by squeezing it for a beat and then releasing it. To half halt in the saddle, stop following his motion with your seat and back for a beat while you squeeze with your calf muscles and squeeze your fingers on the reins. Then, release and follow him again. You will find that he hesitates a tiny bit and gives to your command by rounding himself up into a shorter stride. This is the beginning of collection under saddle.

You can also teach your horse to bend in one direction and then transfer his shape to bend in the opposite direction by working on **serpentines**. This also helps with collection. To do this, simply make a half circle in one direction, go straight for two strides to straighten out the horse, and then ask him to make a half circle in the other direction. Making this change of direction really makes him concentrate on your cues, but remember to use those two strides in between to give him a chance to straighten out, or he will be confused and sloppy in his response when you ask for the new direction.

Spiral down and spiral out exercises at the walk also help to make him more flexible and balanced on curves and help with collection. Start with a twenty-foot circle and the usual bending cues. Then, hold a little more strongly with your outside leg and hand, while you ask a little more definitely for the bend with your inside leg and hand. Let your inside seat bone get a tiny bit more weight in it, but don't collapse your waist to the inside or lean to the inside. Stay in the center of your horse. You will find that he starts to spiral down to a smaller circle. Keep him on the bend and make the circle smaller still on the next revolution. Then, begin the spiral back out to the original twenty-foot circle. Just open your outside rein a little away from his neck and release the hold of your outside leg a little, while you change your seat bone pressure to put a little more weight onto the outside seat bone. Keep asking for the bend with your inside leg and hand, but do it more lightly. He should start to spiral out onto a larger circle. Don't let him go off onto a straight line. Keep that bend. This is a difficult exercise for a green horse, so don't overdo it and don't expect perfection the first time. If he gives you one good spiral in and out, stop on a good note and go to practicing something else. Be sure to reward him with a pat and kind word when he has done well.

HOW CAN YOU USE GROUND POLES AND CAVALLETTI TO HELP YOUR HORSE EXTEND AND COLLECT HIS STRIDE UNDER SADDLE AT THE WALK?

Remember those simple exercises you worked through so patiently on the lunge line with the ground poles and cavalletti? Well, you can now do the same thing at the walk under saddle, following the same procedure, building up from one ground pole to several ground poles and one cavalletti to several cavalletti, spaced either for extension or collection. Since he is already familiar with the exercises from the lunge line work, your horse should get the idea pretty easily. These exercises should, of course, be done for only a short period of time in one lesson. You will find, though, that they sure do make a difference in your horse's attention and performance and consistency of performance. You can even set up a couple of poles on one end of the arena for collection and a couple more at the other end for extension, if you have the space to adjust his stride between sets of poles. Remember, though, this is a more advanced exercise, so don't try to do too much in one day.

Before you go on to chapter 5 and the work at the trot, there are two more things to work on at the walk: the square halt and, for Western riders, the neck rein.

HOW DOES THE RIDER ACHIEVE THE QUIET, SQUARE HALT?

At this point, you are still working with two hands. Remember the half halt mentioned earlier? This little cue will help your horse to stop quietly and evenly. First, pay attention to the feel of the horse under you. As you feel his hind end moving into his front end, half halt for one stride strongly enough to get a firm and distinct pause in his forward motion. Some horses are very light and others are heavy. You have to read his response as light and easy or heavy and slow or somewhere in between. If he doesn't stop on the first try, release and ask again. Don't just pull on him. He's stronger than you anyway. Insist with repeated half halts until he comes to a full halt, even if he's not square yet. Circle him first, if he's not paying attention and try from the circle. Sit very quietly on him and count to five or ten or eight or six seconds or whatever in your head. Start with a low number, because he probably won't stand still very long anyway and you want to give him the idea that you are asking him to move off again, not that he is walking away from your command to halt. Increase the number of seconds he must be still gradually, so that he learns that he must stay quiet for as long as you ask. Then, practice varying the number of seconds, so he has to pay attention to you instead of walking off when he thinks you should be ready. Use the voice commands you used on the lunge line, if you need to. You can eliminate them gradually later.

Only when he has learned to halt can you refine the halt and really make it square. Feel the horse as he walks under you, each hip into the opposite shoulder and rein. To make him square, follow that motion in the walk stride with your half halt cue: left hip into right rein squeeze and right hip into left rein squeeze. Then, release the cue. Soon, he will stop more evenly, with his legs more squarely under him and you will be able to make your half halt cue lighter and less pronounced. Eventually, all you will need to do is give him a light half halt first as a warning for one stride and then on the next stride just stop your back and seat motion, close your legs, and squeeze your fingers, and he will halt in that one stride. Practice getting lighter and more subtle in your cues, so that your halt in the show ring looks like you didn't do anything at all from the judge's perspective.

The last item to work on at the walk is the Western neck rein technique.

HOW DOES THE RIDER TEACH THE HORSE TO NECK REIN?

So far, you have been working with two hands. Start to teach the neck rein from the circle. Remember the inside hand and leg cues that create the circle? Remember the outside leg that holds the shape of the circle and the outside hand that does the same? Okay, walk a circle and use the circle cues. Gradually, remove the inside rein cue and ask the horse to keep the bend with the outside rein cue instead, that is the neck rein. Keep the leg cues the same. In neck reining, be sure to lay the outside rein against the neck between the horse's withers and the crest of his neck, no higher. Start with the rein rather short and gradually let the horse slip the reins through your fingers to make them a little longer and a little longer and a little longer, until he is responding just to the weight of your fingers on the loops of reins and finally just to the weight of the reins alone. You are still using the same principle of inside leg into outside rein, just like you have been all along. The difference is that you have just taught the horse that he can balance himself with fewer cues and lighter cues. Now, you are ready to transfer the reins to one hand, Western style, and ride him not only on the circle with a looser rein but eventually on the rail as well and through all of the other exercises mentioned above. If he gets sloppy on you or starts to turn his nose to the outside of a bend or circle, just go back to using two hands and to teaching him about neck reining on the circle again as a review, and he'll straighten up his act.

HOW SHOULD THE WESTERN RIDER HOLD THE REINS FOR NECK REINING?

If he is working Texas style, he places both reins in his left hand, thumb up, free ends of the reins secured between his thumb and index finger, and excess free rein hanging down the horse's left shoulder. He may put one finger between the reins, if he likes. California style riders pick up the reins with the bit end coming up through the palm with their knuckles up and then secure the reins in a closed fist, allowing the little finger and ring finger to communicate gentle squeezes on the reins to the horse's mouth. The excess free ends of the reins are held in a closed right fist which lies quietly on the rider's right thigh. Either way, the rider subtly follows the horse's neck and head motion with his hand and arm, letting just the weight of the loops of reins between his hand and the bit to be his contact with the horse's mouth. To turn a corner, he simply uses his wrist like a hinge from left to right. To halt, the Texas rider tilts his wrist and hand back toward his body, then releases. The California rider closes his little and ring fingers on the reins in a squeeze. Then, he releases.

Now, whether Western or hunt seat, you should be ready for the trot, chapter 5.

DEVELOPING THE HORSE AND RIDER
TEAM AT THE TROT AND JOG

So far, you have taught your horse how to work correctly on the lunge line and under saddle at the walk. You have worked hard, always remembering those key words: **patience, planning, and persistence**. All of your hard work is starting to pay off. Your horse is more supple, balanced, and obedient, and he is happy in his work. As a rider, you too feel more confident and at ease in communicating with him through your seat, legs, and hands. Now you are ready for the next step, building the trot for hunt seat riders or the jog for Western riders.

HOW DO YOU PREPARE YOUR HORSE TO WORK UNDER SADDLE AT THE TROT OR JOG?

You probably already have some idea of the answer to this question, since developing the walk step by step in chapter 4. As you might have guessed, your horse must learn to trot correctly **on the lunge line** before you can work him successfully under saddle. Here's how you can teach him to develop his muscles and his mind properly in this gait.

First, warm him up without side reins on the lunge line, but this time, let him walk and trot freely about seven or eight minutes in each direction. Then, attach the side reins and spend about five minutes walking him to focus him on the work at hand. Then, to ask him to trot, half-halt the lunge line gently just as his inside hind leg is coming forward. At the same instant, take one step toward his hip, point the lunge whip at his hip and say, "trot" or "come, trot" or whatever command you plan to use. Also remember to use the same tone of voice each time you ask. He should strike off into the trot, but that's just where the problems could begin, so plan and proceed carefully. Here's what to look for in his movement and his attitude.

Most green horses have one of two problems at the trot or jog. Either they want to rush the trot and speed around or they want to dawdle and drift back into a walk. Your first problem to solve, then, will be keeping him consistent at the pace (rhythm) you need to develop in him, whether it be the English trot or the Western jog. If he rushes, use little half-halts every other stride to remind him to adjust his pace. You may even have to make his circle a little smaller at the beginning of this work to keep his mind on you and to prevent him from rushing off on a bigger circle into the canter. If he dawdles, encourage him by pointing the whip at his hip and repeating the voice command, "trot." For some horses, you may need to snap the whip at his hock level, without actually touching him with the lash part of it. Don't overdo your command, though, or he may overreact and begin rushing. Then, you will have to calm him down again. Read your horse's attitude and rhythm carefully. Use the skills you learned in chapter 4 to teach him consistency. Perceive the pace you want and insist that he learn to maintain it over a series of lessons, about fifteen minutes long for each lesson.

All of this may sound pretty basic until you consider the next problem. What about his head and his frame, the shape of his spine? As he began to trot, you probably noticed that he raised his head suddenly and then lowered it again, gradually, as he trotted the circle. Chewing on the bit a little, he relaxed his lower jaw and adjusted the shape of his spine to allow himself to travel comfortably within the limits you have set for him through the side reins. Maybe he even tried to lower his head way down and poke his nose way out. He discovered he needed to learn to keep the trot or jog and his frame at the same time. Why does he need to adjust himself? Didn't he already learn how to carry himself at the walk? Well, yes, but the trot brings more energy and speed and a different rhythm pattern in his footfalls. He must keep his balance in a new way, and he needs a little time to learn to carry himself properly and comfortably. That's why you need to work him on the lunge line before you work under saddle.

Once again, remember, all of these new demands on his muscles and mind can be very tiring for him, so after about ten to fifteen minutes of work at the trot or jog (seven or eight in each direction) with side reins, stop working and spend the rest of your work time under saddle each day. Work at the walk, until you think he is consistent enough at the trot or jog on the lunge line to graduate him to working this new gait under saddle. In fact, once you have begun working him at the walk under saddle, you can start teaching him to trot or jog on the lunge line, so that his lunge line work is always a week or so ahead of the work he is able to do under saddle. That way, his development will be continuous under saddle and you won't lose any training and riding time by moving too slowly with him.

WHAT ABOUT EXTENSION AND COLLECTION AND USING TROTTING POLES AND CAVALLETTI AT THE TROT OR JOG? WHAT ABOUT TRANSITIONS AND SQUARE HALTS?

First, let's deal with trotting poles and cavalletti, because this work not only makes your horse pay attention and stride consistently, but it also allows you to teach him to extend and collect his stride. You learned about this when you worked him at the walk for the same purpose. Once again, go back to the advice and procedures explained in chapter 4. Apply these same principles of step-by-step lessons to advance his skill at the trot or jog: first the warmup with no side reins; then, trotting with the side reins on the flat as just explained; then, trotting over ground poles first without side reins and next with side reins; and finally, trotting over cavalletti first without and then with the side reins. Remember to limit the number of minutes to a total of fifteen for each lesson. However, instead of spacing the poles and cavalletti two feet apart, as you did at the walk, place them four to four and one half feet apart for trotting work. Adjust them to suit your horse's natural stride and the size of the stride you need, a little farther apart for the longer stride of the English trot and a little closer together for the smaller stride of the Western jog. From this basic position, move them up to six inches farther apart for extension work and up to six inches closer together for collection work.

But wait! What about the difference between the Western jog and the English trot? Basically, the two are a matter of the shape of the horse's spine and the degree of collection versus extension, not just a matter of slow versus fast or long versus short stride. The horse's entire spine and thus his whole frame is either more or less round. At the Western jog, his spine is rounded in a long, low frame with the pole of his head level with his withers. His back hooves track up to his front hoof prints, showing that he is using his back and hindquarter muscles, but the stride is soft, relaxed, and compressed (rounded). At the English trot, he looks longer and more springy. He takes bigger strides forward. He may carry his head higher, only because his spine and whole frame are shaped in a higher arc, not because he is hollowing his back and raising his head to avoid contact with the bit. He moves willingly from behind into the bit. He tracks up behind like the Western horse, but his stride is longer and has more action than a horse moving in a Western jog. For both English and Western horses, the horse must move forward from behind into the bit. The horse must relax his lower jaw and carry the bit, softly keeping his face on a vertical (or almost vertical) plane, as he balances the energy coming forward from his hindquarter movement. Keep your eyes open as you work your horse and learn to see his movement in terms of his whole frame, not just parts of it. Let yourself feel his rhythm and watch for changes. Keep his attention and use your voice, whip, and hand on the line to help him along. In other words, be patient, be perceptive, and be persistent.

Should the English horse learn to collect? Certainly? Should the Western horse learn to extend? Absolutely. Just make sure he keeps the shape you want. Putting these various "gears" into your horse's repertoire of skills will make him more supple and balanced. This added variation will also keep the brilliance and sharp, crisp quality in his stride for show ring performance. Last but not least, it will keep him from getting into a rut and becoming bored with his work. Besides, once you are working under saddle, you will be amazed at how finely tuned and easy to handle he becomes when you are able to collect or extend his stride at will, with only gentle touches from your seat, legs, and hands.

Okay, so much for extensions and collections and trotting poles and cavalletti.

WHAT ABOUT WALK TO TROT AND TROT TO WALK TRANSITIONS?

WHAT ABOUT TROT TO SQUARE HALT AND HALT TO TROT TRANSITIONS?

Each time you ask for the trot from the walk, or the walk from the trot, your horse will become smoother in his upward and downwards transitions and grow stronger in physical and mental ability to keep his shape or frame as he changes gaits. That does not mean, however, that you should nag at him and work the transition practice to death, making him change gaits every four or six strides. Getting too pushy now only mixes him up and breeds resistance. Let him get the hang of transitions gradually, as with everything else you do. Do a few each lesson, spending a few minutes working just on this part of his performance. Ask once every dozen strides or so and work down to once every six or eight strides. You will find that his upwards transitions improve faster than his downwards ones, simply because coming down requires him to have more mental concentration and more controlled use of his hindquarters to keep himself from diving down onto his forehand. Just give him time, make sure your commands are correct, and be careful to keep him focused on the task you ask him to perform. If he rushes, make the circle smaller and use half halts to keep his attention. If he is sloppy, use half halts and the whip cue as needed to make his responses crisper and lighter.

Only after he has mastered walk/trot and trot/walk transitions should you expect him to have the strength, coordination, and concentration to perfect trot/halt and halt/trot transitions. When you do ask for a halt, you should expect him to stand quietly at attention for up to ten seconds before you move him off again. When you ask him to move from the halt to the trot, he should do so smoothly and crisply, with just a gentle cue from you. Remember also, that the next problem, the square halt, cannot be accomplished until he is willing to pay attention to begin with. So, the next logical question is:

HOW DO YOU TEACH HIM TO HALT SQUARELY FROM THE TROT?

The most common problem at this point is that the horse stops okay, but his feet are every which way. Sometimes he looks like he stopped in the middle of a trot stride. Other times, he breaks first to the walk and sort of wanders into a halt on his forehand. Both problems take practice to correct.

First, you practice getting him to halt and then move on to a trot without the side reins. He will probably look pretty sloppy, as described above, not pretty and rounded, with his head in the right position and all four feet squarely under himself when he stops. As you begin work with the side reins, however, you will find that he improves, because he is learning to keep his shape and stop better at the same time. Despite the side reins, however, he may still not figure out completely by himself that he needs to get his butt under himself and stop with his hind legs under him, so he won't fall onto his forehand.

HOW DO YOU HELP HIM PUT HALT AND ROUNDNESS TOGETHER?

You are certainly going to need this roundness when he halts under saddle to prevent him from falling on his forehand and "running through your hands," that is leaning into the bit. As he is trotting, pick a moment when he is really paying attention well. As his inside hind leg comes up, lower the hand holding the lunge line and half halt the line as you say "ready." The very next stride (or no more than two strides later, if you can't get the timing just right yourself yet) half-halt again and say,"whoa" of "ho." You will be surprised to see that just giving him a warning and helping him with a half halt can make all the difference in getting across the idea of stopping squarely with all four feet under him while keeping his shape (frame). Make sure you release between half halts and after he has stopped. Never drag on him. Stay crisp and light, and he will learn to work the same way. You will also find that working walk to trot and trot to walk transitions before you teach the square halt will prepare his muscles and his mind and make teaching the square halt easier.

After all of this careful practice on the lung line, you and your horse should finally be ready to work at the trot or jog under saddle.

HOW DOES THE RIDER DEVELOP AN EVEN, BALANCED, CONSISTENT TROT OR JOG UNDER SADDLE?

Always remember the obvious. Before you can expect to teach your horse anything, you must be correct in your position in the saddle. Go back and review the seat, legs, and hand positions that mean proper communication and harmony with your horse. Next, consider that warm up and review must be completed at the walk before you even begin to trot. Remember to work two-handed during your warmup, even if you are a Western rider. Take five or ten minutes to do the following:

1.   Let your horse stretch out on a loose rein and lengthen his walk freely under saddle along the rail. Remember, always stretch out before you expect anything further. You did the same thing in chapter four under saddle and on the lunge line before you attached the side reins to your horse's bridle, so let your horse stretch out. Then, take the reins up to normal working position.

2. Gradually begin to make circles, large ones first, then smaller ones, in both directions at various places in the arena. Gently work a few spiral in and spiral out circles.

3. Change the circles to serpentines and figure eights.

4. Walk over a couple of poles and cavalletti a few times in each direction.

5. Ask for some collection on the circle and some lengthening on the rail. Vary the spot where you ask for each, such as a circle on a corner and a lengthening down the long side of the arena the first time, but a circle half way down the long side and a lengthening on the short side of the arena the next time. Work both directions.

6. Ask for walk to halt and halt to walk transitions.

7. If you are a Western rider, you can take a few minutes to review neck reining at the walk, but be sure to go back to two hands when the time comes to begin the trot. You can always teach your horse to neck rein at the jog. In fact, once he has his jog down to the frame and rhythm you want, he should carry the idea of neck reining over into the trot pretty easily.

One last reminder: All the while you are riding, pay attention to your own position in the saddle and how accurately you are communicating with your horse.
Now, you should be ready to begin work at the trot or jog.

One walking stride before you actually ask for the trot or jog, half halt your horse just a little, to let him know a change is coming, like the word "ready" and the half halt prepared him on the lunge line. In fact, you can even use the same verbal command to help him get the idea of what you want. The next stride, ask for trot by opening your chest a little. This will help you engage your seat bones, so you can give your horse a little scoop with them. At the same instant, squeeze gently with both calf muscles and allow your hands to follow his neck and head as he springs up into the trot. Then, quietly allow your body to follow his motion.

If he strikes off too hard, maybe you asked too harshly. If your cues were light but he still reacted too much, try asking him on a small circle first, to keep his attention on his work instead of on racing away at the trot. Use a soothing voice to calm him.

If he is sluggish, ask a little more strongly but practice with him so that he learns to respond to lighter and lighter cues. One way to do this is to carry a 39-inch dressage. Just when you ask him to trot, if he ignores your leg cue, tap him with the whip right behind your calf. This must be done instantly right after the leg cue. He should move off at the trot. You may need to practice with the whip for a few lessons to teach him that he must respect the light touch of your calf muscles as a cue to move forward. Gradually, you can stop using the whip cue altogether. Of course, you can use your voice to reinforce your leg and seat aids, but don't start yelling at him. This will just confuse him. One firm word can do wonders when said at just the right time. That right time is just when the whip taps him, sort of like saying, "Get the point, pal?" Always be sure to reward him with a kind word and a pat when he does well.

This trot or jog is supposed to be smooth, fluid, balanced, rhythmic. Rider and horse should move as one being. But what if it doesn't turn out that way? How will you ever get to bending, transitions, extension, and collection? And what about that halt under saddle? Wait! Not so fast! Remember, one step at a time. Let's look at the problems you can run into just getting him to move consistently and getting yourself to ride in harmony with him.

If you are lucky, he will give you a reasonably relaxed, consistent trot and use his hindquarters to move forward into the bit as he did on the lunge line with the side reins. What if, instead, he raises his head, hollows his back away from your seat, and proceeds to pound along in a rush, bouncing you like a ping pong ball on his back? If his back is hollow and his trot is rushed, rise to it, rather than bouncing along making both you and your horse uncomfortable. Rise to it? Post the trot, even if you are riding in a Western saddle? You may have to, until he is willing to stretch down, engage his hindquarters, relax, and move forward more fluidly. This may take one circle, several circles, or ten minutes. Happily, the work on the lunge line should have prepared him quite a bit, so that this type of problem is less severe and lasts only a circle or two, until you have his attention at the new gait. If he is a confirmed racer at the trot under saddle, you will just have to work with him more on the lunge line first to prepare him and to work the edge off of him.

Your horse, though, may not be the only problem. Maybe you are communicating a desire to rush without even being aware of it. Do you dig your heels into him without meaning to at the trot? Go back to the information on position, get your leg in the right place, and concentrate on keeping your heels out of his sides. What if you grab tightly with your thighs as you lean forward and grip the reins to help you keep your balance? This position will hardly make him feel relaxed. If anything, it will make him want to panic. Work on your position at the walk and be sure you don't go into a "desperate death grip" as soon as he moves into trot. Maybe you lean backwards instead, bouncing on his kidneys, sitting behind his action, with your legs in front of you. How can you expect him to relax, when your seat is driving him from behind, screaming, "Go! Go! Go!"? Correct position in the saddle makes for correct communication and improved performance. If you need work, maybe you even need to work on a different horse a few times, one that will be more patient and calm while you get the feel of how to sit correctly at the trot.

It is also very important that you can feel how to get your diagonals correctly for posting by sensing what is happening in your seat, legs, and lower back, NOT by looking down at the horse's shoulder to see which shoulder is up or down on a given beat. Looking down at him is like driving a car by staring at the hood or front fender instead of looking out at the road ahead. Better to look ahead of you as you ride and feel the trot this way.

Rely on the horse's inside hind leg to help you. At the two-beat trot, your horse's legs move in diagonal pairs. As your horse's inside hind leg and outside foreleg (front leg) are traveling forward, you feel your seat and lower back moving toward the outside of the circle. Why? Well, his inside hip is rising as his inside hind leg comes forward. Thus, he tosses you toward the other side of his body and toward the outside of the circle. When this happens, you should be sitting to the trot, so that you don't throw him off balance. He is supposed to be bent into the shape of the circle, so how can he stay bent one way if you rise to the trot the other way and over weight him in the opposite direction?

When do you rise to the trot? On the next beat, of course, when the outside hind leg and the inside foreleg (front) leg are tossing your body weight back into the inside shape of the circle. Sit the trot on a quiet, schooled horse some time and just feel what is happening: inside to outside; outside to inside. Simple, isn't it? If you let the horse's motion tell you when to rise and sit you will never make a mistake on diagonals, and you will never have to do that silly action of looking down at the horse to see what you should be able to feel in the first place.

In fact, as you get even better at feeling the horse's motion through your seat and lower back, you can even start the horse on the correct diagonal and rise to the very first beat of the trot in an upwards transition from walk to trot. Just feel when he is ready to move your seat from the outside toward the inside with his hip and leg. At that moment, cue for the trot with the usual cue described in this chapter, and he will strike off just as you are rising. Just be sure you don't start to rise until he actually begins to change gaits, or you will be ahead of his motion. When your cues and your timing match his body movements in this way, such a smooth transition can really impress a judge looking for a polished performance in the show ring in English classes. Using this technique at the Western jog will also put more polish on a Western horse and rider team, who must move as one, especially in pleasure classes. Knowing just what beat on which your horse begins to jog really helps you to follow his motion softly with your seat and lower back. No more getting jarred into the trot or left behind a beat in following your horse's rhythm.

What's more, since you can feel his rhythm and the placement of his footfalls through your seat and lower back, you can time your half-halts to match his rhythm, and thus be more effective in getting a correct response from him just when you need it. For example, in creating bends and circles, use your leg, seat, or hand (Western or English) for a turning cue right on the beat when the horse's trot step makes him bend to the inside of the circle, that is, when his inside hind leg is coming up. That way, his body is ready to respond to your cue, and his response is so natural that he almost thinks that it was his own idea in the first place. You can see how such good timing makes for a lot less resistance to your signals on the part of the horse. Release the cue on the next beat and go back to following his motion. Then, cue again for the next "inside" beat. This "cue/release" method keeps his attention on you sharp and prevents him from wanting to lean on your hands or bulge one side of his body out against your leg to resist your signals. Cue for a half-halt in the English trot only as you are coming down from posting to sitting position. Thus, you will be able to use your seat and lower back and not just your legs to cue the horse more effectively and will be able to feel his response more precisely.

Now that you have the basic problem of the upwards transition to the trot and the problem of feeling the horse's movement, you can begin to create some consistency at the trot or jog. Remember how you used circles, spirals, serpentines, and half-halts at the walk? Well, now it is up to you to create a similar plan at the trot or jog, always working to encourage your horse to maintain the frame or shape you want as well as to attain the rhythm you want. Go back and review chapter 4 and its suggested routines. Then, go back to the beginning of this chapter and reread the reminders for working your horse at the walk under saddle in preparation for the trot or jog. Set up a similar plan of exercises at the trot or jog. Practice you new work at this new gait for about ten or fifteen minutes in the middle of your schooling session, after you have had a chance to do warmup and review. Then, near the end of the lesson, go back and review things your horse can do well, in order to finish your lesson on a good note. Praise your horse for doing well. If you and your horse have been working carefully together, it won't take too many days for him at least to give you a reasonably consistent trot or jog for five to ten minutes straight. If he is a little stiffer working in one direction, work a few minutes more on the bad direction in each lesson. When you ask for downwards transitions from the trot to the walk or the trot to the halt under saddle, don't be too picky yet. Just be happy that he is willing to give and come down when you ask. You will develop his square halt from the trot a little later here. Of course, if you are a Western rider, once you feel that he is paying attention at the jog and giving you a steady rhythm, you can begin to teach him to neck rein at the jog just as you did earlier at the walk

Now, it will be time to address the next question.

HOW DOES THE RIDER DEVELOP DEGREES OF EXTENSION AND COLLECTION AT THE WALK OR JOG?

Since he already has the idea of extension and collection from work on the lunge line and from work at the walk under saddle, this should be a pretty easy task for the both of you. In fact, it may be easier for your horse to respond simply because he has more energy and forward motion at the trot than at the walk. Remember, always ask for stretching out before you ask for collection, to avoid cramping his muscles and teaching him bad habits. Remember also, whether you are a Western or an English rider, your horse should have the ability to extend and collect his frame at all gaits. Finally, remember that extension means bigger steps with the same rhythm, not faster steps.

To extend the Western jog or sitting trot, simply use your seat, in rhythm with his stride, to encourage him to take bigger steps. As he reaches under himself more with his hind legs in response to your seat cues, you will feel the energy move into his forehand and will feel it in the reins. Just follow his motion quietly with your body and your hands. Don't restrict him. Remember also, once he gives you bigger steps, don't keep cueing him every stride, or he may become annoyed and either move off into a pounding trot with his head in the air or rush off into the canter. Try to cue with both seat bones evenly, or you may accidentally cue him into the canter. (More about using your seat to get the canter or lope in the next chapter.) If he drops back into smaller steps, cue for the extension again. Try this along the long side of the arena or down the center line. Before you get to the corners or the short side of the arena, use half-halts to gather his stride back to normal again. If he wants to rush off, use circles and serpentines to keep his attention. When he is consistent and balanced enough, he should be able to give you extension all the way around the arena without falling apart and dropping his inside shoulder and rushing through corners.

When he has learned the concept of extension, begin, just as you did at the walk, by using half-halts and circles to ask him to collect his stride. Work circles at the corners of the arena. Then, circle at various places in the arena. Finally, expect him to maintain his collection all the way down one long side and through a corner and then all the way around the arena. Naturally, remember that all of this work is going to take many lessons to teach your horse, not just a day or two, so be patient. Don't try to teach a whole bunch of new things in one lesson. Teach only one new thing in a lesson.

Use ground poles and / or cavalletti, this time set at about four feet apart, to help with extension and / or collection, just as you used them in the walking exercises under saddle and on the lunge line. When you trot over cavalletti, however, you may be wise to lighten your seat and to stand in your stirrups a little to take up the bounce from going over the cavalletti. Just be careful not to overweight your horse's forehand be getting too far forward. Keeping your leg in position with your heel sinking down and keeping your head and chest up will help you avoid this problem. Also, remember to keep your hands low and light and following your horse's motion. Don't grab at him with each bounce to keep your balance, or you will do more harm than good to his training.

Now, you are ready for the next step, the square halt under saddle.

HOW DOES THE RIDER DEVELOP THE SQUARE HALT FROM THE TROT OR JOG UNDER SADDLE?

Many or the principles you and your horse have already learned will apply to this task, but this new gait makes for its own unique problems. The horse is moving forward with more energy. In addition, his feet are moving in diagonal pairs, and things are just happening faster than at the walk. Still, with a little practice, perception, and patience, you will be able to feel his rhythm and ask him to learn what you are trying to teach him without pulling or yanking on his mouth to bring him down from the trot or jog to a square halt.

Once again, it's a good idea to start teaching this new idea from a circle in a smaller area, like the corner of the arena and to work on downward transitions to the walk, before you try to teach the halt. First, one stride or perhaps two strides before you want him to give you that downward transition to the halt, give him that "Ready?" signal, the half-halt. Then, using two hands on the reins, held low near his withers, and feeling his motion through your seat, lower back, and legs, ask for a stronger half-halt as the horse is stepping with his inside leg into the shape of the bend. Review trot or jog to walk transitions before you ask for the trot or jog to the halt.

To get the halt, completely stop the motion of your back and seat, close your entire legs from crotch to calf muscles against his sides, and squeeze your fingers on the reins. Sit straight (don't lean backwards) and let your seat sink straight down. This time, don't release the resistance until the horse has completed the second beat of the trot stride. You are, thus, holding the half-halt for a whole stride before releasing it and using your seat to make the horse lower his hindquarters and get his hind legs under himself. This action on your part will give your horse time to step up into your resistance to his motion with all of his legs. Thus, he has a better chance of stopping squarely. Keep your hands low, and remember to release the resistance in your body after one stride. If he does not come to a halt, ask again in a couple of strides, this time with a sharper and stronger cue. Caution. Do not DRAG on the reins or hold the cue for more than one stride. All cues or aids — seat, legs, and hands — should be crisp, not long and drawn out. You are giving a signal, not pulling taffy. If you hold your cue for more than one stride, your horse will just learn to resist more strongly instead of learning to give and then relax. All you will be teaching him is how to pull on you. Guess who wins in that tug of war?

If he listens, praise him and insist that he stay still for a few seconds. The next time you try the halt, try to see if he will re-spond to a lighter cue. Try to get your cues lighter and less notice-able, so that your performance as a team will look smooth and effortless to a judge in the show ring. If you are a Western rider, practice the halt with two hands before you do it single-handed, neck rein fashion.

Try to feel through your seat and legs whether the horse has stopped with his feet squarely under himself. If not, try gently to use a light squeeze with your right leg, if his right hip and right hind leg are stretched out behind him and your left leg if his left is stretched out. Resist just enough with your hands to prevent him from moving forward with his front end. Release as soon as he has taken a step forward with the necessary hind leg and has agreed to stand quietly. If one of his forelegs is a step too far for-ward, once he has halted, just resist a little more with the hand on that side, until he moves his front foot back to square. Be care-ful. Often all you may need to do is to vibrate your fingertips gently on that rein to get him to give. Don't overdo your cues. Go back to neutral as soon as he responds, or he will end up raising his head, stepping too far back, or even wiggling himself all out of line to get free of your heavyhandedness.

If his halt is crooked, with one hip to the side, ask yourself if you applied your leg pressure evenly in both legs. Maybe, though, he just has a habit of avoiding the pressure or of being fussy. In that case, you will need to drop your leg on his problem side back a little and maybe even hold it a little stronger as you come to a halt. Do this a few times and see if he gets the idea to keep his body straight. If not, try stopping him next to a wall or rail, so that he can't swing his hip out of line on that side. Insist that he stand at attention at the halt, until you ask him to move on, be it five seconds or fifteen seconds. Get a helper on the ground to tell you how squarely he has stopped, if you are still having trouble feeling his position through your body.

To move from the halt to the trot, just use your "forward" cues a little more strongly and crisply at first. Sometimes tapping him behind your leg with a dressage whip just as you ask can help him make his response quicker and lighter. He will soon get the idea that you want a halt to trot and not just a halt to walk. If he has stopped squarely, the spring up into the trot from the halt will be easy and balanced for him. However, if he has not learned to stop squarely, that upwards transition from halt to trot will lack lightness and balance. Remember, review what he already knows and give him time for his muscles and his mind to develop and polish his performance. He can't learn everything in one lesson. Besides, he will, like anybody, have good days and bad days, days when his attention isn't what it should be, days when he seems to forget what he should know. On bad days, go back to basics a little more. Then, when you ask for work on a movement he is just learning, you will get less resistance and more attention and "try" out of him. Be patient; be persistent; be perceptive of his mood and reactions. Get a helper on the ground to tell you how squarely he has stopped, if you are still having trouble feeling his position through your body. That person should also keep an eye on your cues to see that you are not the one creating the problem.

Now comes the next question:

HOW DOES THE RIDER SWITCH DIAGONALS SMOOTH-LY WHEN HE IS RISING (POSTING) TO THE TROT?

Suppose the rider makes a circle and wants to change direction in the arena? Suppose he wants to make an X across the arena and to change his diagonal in the center of the X? How does he make the change without disturbing the horse's balance or the flow of his stride? Simple. As the rider comes down into the saddle from posting or rising position, he just sits one extra beat or step. That way, when he rises the next time, he will be rising to the opposite diagonal from the one he started on. If you need to, you can have a friend on the ground watch you practice changing diagonals, if you have trouble feeling the individual beats or steps of the trot. Once you can feel the horse's motion accurately in your seat, lower back, and legs, though, as described earlier in this chapter, you should be able to pick up the change of diagonals pretty easily. Just don't get tense or impatient with yourself. If you do, your horse will sense the tension and become upset too. Don't communicate "bad vibes." Think and work positively and patiently.

Now you are almost ready to begin work at the canter with your horse. Just a few closing reminders in this chapter and you will be on your way to chapter 6. Remember, since the horse's stride has more speed and energy at the trot, he can sometimes get away from you like a locomotive going downhill. If he tends to charge down the long side of the arena at a pounding trot and tends to take his corners like a car leaning on two wheels, use circles and half-halts to help him develop consistency all the way around the arena. If, instead, he gets lazy and sluggish and slows

down like a car running out of gas, use light taps with your dressage whip to encourage him to use his hindquarters, as you cue
him with your calf muscles. Remember to cue and then to follow
his motion to see how many strides he will give you of the trot or
jog you want. Remind him when he begins to drag. Don't keep
jabbing at him every stride, or you will end up with a "dead-sid-
ed" horse who doesn't respond to your leg at all. He will simply
learn to ignore the constant nagging. As you and your horse develop proficiency as a team at the trot, you will finally become
ready to begin work at the canter or lope. Onward to chapter 6!

DEVELOPING THE HORSE AND RIDER TEAM AT THE CANTER AND LOPE

After all of the patient work you and your horse have been through in previous chapters on the lunge line and under saddle at the walk and the trot, you should be well-prepared for work at the English canter or at the Western lope. What's more, you will find that, as you and your horse have become physically and mentally atuned to the job, learning something new becomes even easier. Naturally, before you try anything new under saddle, as you know, you must first teach your horse on the lunge line. Therefore, here's the first important question of this chapter:

WHAT LUNGE LINE WORK MUST BE DONE TO DEVELOP AN EVEN, CONSISTENT CANTER OR LOPE IN WHICH THE HORSE MOVES FROM BEHIND INTO THE BIT?

In order to keep your horse's training moving smoothly, you can begin lunge line work at the canter while you are finishing trotting work under saddle. Usually about a week or two before you plan to do serious work under saddle at the canter or lope, you can begin preparing your horse for this work through lunge line exercises described below here. By now, you must have guessed that warmup and review play an important part in getting both you and your horse set physically and mentally. The lunge line will prepare your horse and allow you to watch how he is responding on a given work day.

Before you begin the exercises that follow here, remember a few guidelines.

1. Warm up without side reins for five or ten minutes before you attach side reins. If your horse is very fresh, maybe you should turn him out to play in the field for an hour or so before working him.

2. Work on the flat before you do any work over poles or caval-letti.

3. Review old, familiar exercises before you try anything new.

4. Be patient, persistent, and perceptive.

5. Finish the lesson with something your horse can do easily, and praise him well for his work.

Okay, here's how the lunge line exercise work should proceed. Begin with your horse at the Western jog or at the English trot, whichever way you have taught him to perform. First, review lengthening and collection as well as walk to trot and trot to walk transitions. Next review trot to halt and halt to trot transitions. Work first without and then with side reins. Then, work with trotting poles and/or cavalletti.

It is very important that your horse be performing correctly before you add a new move, or the mistakes your horse was making at the slower gaits will be magnified at the faster gait. Remember, if something is consistently going wrong at a faster gait, always backtrack to a slower pace to fix the problem. Then, once the problem has been corrected, move back up to the faster gait. Thus, if your horse is still having a particular trotting problem, like dropping his shoulder on corners or rushing around, don't expect it to go away when he begins to canter. Things will just be worse at the canter, until you help him to fix his problem at the trot.

Once you are sure the horse is performing at his best at the walk, trot, and halt, take him to one corner of the arena. Lunge him in a twenty or thirty foot circle at the trot. Let the walls of the arena or the rails on two sides help your horse keep his shape on the circle and make him aware that he can't go flying off on a straight line away from you at the canter or lope, once you ask for an upwards transition. When you do ask, be sure to ask as he is headed into the corner. That way, he will think more of his balance on the circle and his transition and less about just flying off at speed. Gradually, you can start working at another place in the arena, without using the corner for help.

OKAY, HOW DO YOU ASK FOR THE CANTER OR LOPE AND WHY DO YOU ASK FROM THE TROT FIRST AND NOT FROM THE WALK FIRST?

Let's answer the second question first. It is easier for your horse to move from trot to canter or lope than from walk to canter or lope, because he already has some momentum and doesn't need to work as hard to make the change.

Before you try to follow the directions below here on how to ask, also be sure, of course, that you are able to determine what lead your horse is on when you watch him canter. What shoulder and side of his body is he leading with? He should be leading with the side of his body that is on the inside of the circle. The forehand (front leg) and hindquarter (hind leg) on the inside should be moving a little ahead of those on the outside. Get someone to help you watch for this, if you have trouble catching the horse's motion. (Reading the directions below carefully and watching your horse move freely in the pasture will help develop your horseman's eye, too, in this important observation.) If the horse's forehand is leading on one side but his hind leg is leading on the other side, he is cross-cantering. Don't let him do this on the lunge line or under saddle. Bring him back to the trot and prepare to try again. Maybe he got excited, maybe you gave him the wrong cue, or maybe he has a bad habit of cross-cantering. As you proceed with this chapter, you will see how to teach him to respond as you expect him to.

Now for that first question that we mentioned just above. Here's how you should ask for the canter or lope and what type of reactions you might get. Remember half-halting the lunge line and cuing your horse when his inside hind leg is coming forward? Okay. Once his trot is at the pace and shape (frame) you want, ask for the canter or lope by giving a little squeeze or half-halt on the line and pointing at his hip with your whip at the same instant the inside hind leg is coming forward. By doing this, you will ensure that he will strike off on the correct lead with both the front and back of his body (forehand and hindquarter).

Before we proceed with any further directions, let's examine what steps the horse actually takes in a canter stride and how he starts his body moving into the canter. What is the order of the footfalls at the canter or lope? For a right lead canter, the horse takes the three steps or beats of the canter stride as follows: first he starts with his left hind leg; then he steps with his left front and right hind legs together; and finally, he reaches out with his right front or leading leg as the third and final beat or step of the canter or lope stride. If he is to be on the left lead, he starts with his right hind, then goes to his left hind and right front together, and finally reaches out with his left front or leading leg.

WHY IS THE ORDER OF FOOTFALLS SO IMPORTANT, AND HOW DOES IT CONNECT TO THE INSIDE HIND LEG CUE?

As the horse's inside hind leg comes forward, you cue him, right? Okay. So now he takes a bigger step forward with that inside hind leg as a response to your cue. This bigger step puts him out of balance. He is too far forward, so he has to catch up to restore his balance at a new, more forward, center of gravity by using his next step to move up to the next faster gait, the canter or lope. Think about it. His next step, after you cue him on the inside hind leg, will be with the outside hind leg. Since he will be trying to regain his balance, that next step, with that outside hind leg, will be the first step of the three-beat canter stride. The following step will be the inside hind and outside front legs together, and the last step will be with the inside front, which becomes the leading leg, the one that holds him up as his body goes around the circle in the canter.

WHAT REACTION MAY YOU GET FROM HIM, ONCE HE MOVES INTO THE CANTER OR LOPE?

Although your earlier work at the walk and trot has made him more balanced and responsive, he is not polished at the canter or lope yet. Just getting him to start on the correct lead may be a problem, if he has a habit of cross-leading or traveling on the wrong lead. Remember, if he makes either of these mistakes, bring him back to the trot right away. Get his attention again by getting a correct trot. Then, ask for the canter again. If he keeps making mistakes, have someone who knows what to look for watch you to make sure you are asking at the right moment and in the correct manner. Be sure you and your horse get the cue and the lead correctly before you try to do anything else at the canter. If he won't take the canter at all but insists, instead, on rushing around at the trot, as a response to your canter cue, get his attention back again at the trot. Then, ask for the canter again, carefully. You may want to work only in one corner of the arena for a while. If your cues to him were correct, was he really ready to be asked to canter in the first place? Was he really paying attention? If he is really strung out and rushing around at the trot, practice the spiral in and the spiral out at the trot as explained in earlier chapters at the trot first. He will have something to think about and will have to focus on his body movements more precisely. On his last step of the spiral out, just as his inside hind leg is coming forward, ask for the canter. Another tactic to get his attention is to ask for the canter cue just after he has come out of a set of trotting poles on a circle, as described in chapter five. He will be thinking about where he is placing his feet, and reacting properly to your cue should be easier for him.

Once he takes the actual upwards transition to the canter, he is ready to start developing some consistency of rhythm and correct form or frame. Don't start picking at him on downwards transitions from canter to trot or canter to walk yet. Chances are, they will be sloppy until he gets familiar with traveling the way he should at the canter. Okay, let's help him train his muscles and his mind in the fine points of this new, faster gait.

On the lunge line at the canter the same rules of patience, perception, and persistence apply as in previous work at the walk and trot. Don't ask for too much too fast and don't practice the new movement until he is bored to death or irritated at not being able to please you. Follow the several common sense guidelines given in earlier chapters. Here's how to work on refining his rhythm, balance, and frame (shape).

Watch that canter stride. Is his head up and is he rushing around with his back hollow? As you see his leading leg (inside front) hit the ground, his hind legs will be off the ground. At that instant, give a little half-halt on the line with your hand held low. At the same time, point at his hip with the whip in your other hand. He should reach under himself with his hind legs on his next stride and lower and relax his neck and his head, and his jaw. Be careful not to overdo the whip cue, or he will get more excited instead of more relaxed.

Maybe instead of rushing around, he is dragging along, heavy on his forehand and not using his hind legs strongly enough. He may not be reaching under himself with his hind legs and may even be so sluggish that he is falling apart at the canter and trotting behind while cantering in front. If this is his problem, encourage him with the whip cue to use himself behind. Remember, though, to keep your hand low as you hold the line, or he may decide to raise his head and go blasting off. Help him to find that same low, relaxed, consistent frame and rhythm that he had at the trot by adjusting your whip and half-halt cues accordingly.

Before you attach side reins for canter work, make sure that he is at least able to take the upwards transition cue to canter consistently and to maintain a reasonably steady, relaxed canter around the circle for several revolutions. Then, when you do attach the side reins, his canter will improve even more (over a week or two of schooling, depending on the horse). At this stage, you can start to build extension and collection with ground poles and cavalletti, just as you did before at the trot. This time, though, the poles should be six feet , not four feet, apart. You can start with them at twelve feet to give him a stride in between to think and to adjust his body at this new speed. With this work, you are refining the "gears" on his canter. More extension will give you an English canter; more collection will give you a Western lope.

To make him even more responsive, you can spiral him in and out of his circle at the canter, to make him bend more easily laterally, but don't use ground poles or cavalletti when you are doing spirals. Make sure when you ask him to spiral into a smaller circle or out into a larger circle that you keep him on the shape of the circle and ask him to make a step sideways as he canter forward in time with the movement of his inside hind leg. Also, give a cue only once every other stride, to give him time to think and to adjust his body to your command.

LAST, HOW DO YOU REFINE HIS DOWNWARDS TRANSITIONS?

As his leading (front inside) leg hits the ground, half-halt the line and give him the verbal cue, "trot." Also, lower the pitch of your voice for downwards transitions and raise it for upwards transitions. By half-halting when his leading leg is down and when his hind legs are in the air, you will give him a chance to reach under himself and use his hind end to slow down on the next stride. He won't plop onto his forehand and drop into a hammering trot with his head in the air. Downwards transitions are always harder for the horse to control than upwards transitions, because he has to keep his frame and still control all the power of his body to slow it down. You can help him by setting up some ground poles at the four foot trotting distance, canter him up to about two strides away on the line, and then ask for the downwards transition to trot. He will have to pay attention and watch his feet, so he will learn to carry himself better as he comes down to trot. Otherwise, he will strike his hooves on the poles, because they are spaced for trot, not canter. Be patient with him. When all of this careful work has been done on the lunge line, you will be surprised at how much easier he gets the idea of the kind of canter you expect him to develop under saddle.

Remember also, complete work on trot to canter and canter to trot before you ask for walk to canter and canter to walk. You can use the ground pole setup idea again, this time with the poles set at the two foot walk distance, to bring him down from canter to walk and to keep the walk consistent. Canter to halt should never be tried before all of the previously mentioned work here has been completed. You may need stronger half-halts to bring him from canter to walk or to halt at first and stronger whip cues to bring him from halt to canter or walk to canter, but work patiently as you did every other exercise, and he will develop his body and his mind.

Before you begin work under saddle at the canter, consider these additional tips to help a horse with a special problem. Some horses are so excitable that they want to gallop, buck, and kick out instead of working quietly. If you know your horse is the type who will go ballistic when you begin to canter him on the lunge line, take charge of the situation before it becomes a habitual problem. Turn him out in the field or pasture to play before you work him. Get his focus and attention at the walk and trot on the lunge line and make sure he is thoroughly prepared before you ask for canter. Work in a smaller area at first and one that is free of distractions, so he won't have an excuse to become a runaway freight train.

Suppose the horse keeps taking the wrong lead or keeps cross-cantering, even though you know you have asked him correctly and you know he has gotten the cue. First, rule out injury or chronic health problems. Does this refusal to take the correct lead happen in both directions? Is he just ignoring your cue, or is he trying to tell you he is hurting somewhere? Ask someone who knows to check for lameness you might not see. Check with the vet to see if your horse has a problem only the vet can detect, like early ringbone*, a slightly strained stifle*, or an old injury or splint* acting up. If health problems can be ruled out, your horse simply has an ingrained habit of traveling incorrectly and must be taught a new habit that makes sense to him.

In such a case, try this exercise with ground poles. Set three of them up on a twenty-foot circle, each pole twelve feet from the next, like the spokes of a wheel, as you did in earlier exercises with trotting distances. Ask your horse to trot. Once he steps over the first pole and all four of his legs are in the space between the first and second poles, ask for the canter in the usual way. If he takes the wrong lead, or cross canters, he will strike his hooves on the second and third poles, because they create a bend on the circle and he will be bending out of the circle. This will feel uncomfortable for him, and he will be punishing himself for making the mistake. Bring him gently back to trot as he comes out of the poles, trot him around calmly, and then ask for canter again the same way. He will soon get the point and take the correct lead, because it will be more comfortable for him. You have set up conditions for him to "teach himself," with your kind help. That's a lot easier and productive than yanking on the line and yelling at him angrily. Provide him the opportunity and the reason to learn a new habit, and the new way of going will make sense to him.

Remember the mental level you are dealing with here. The horse cannot think with the complex reasoning that you use. Make things understandable for him at his level and he will get the point with some practice, patience, and persistence on your part.

Now, at last, you are ready to begin work under saddle at the canter or lope.

HOW DOES THE RIDER DEVELOP AN EVEN, BALANCED, CONSISTENT CANTER OR LOPE UNDER SADDLE?

First, before you can teach your horse, be sure that you can sit the canter with your seat in the saddle for all three beats of each canter stride, with your lower back following the horse's motion, with your legs in position but relaxed, and with your hands, arms, and shoulders following the horse's rhythmic strides through a light feel of the reins. If you bounce at the canter or lope or if you must use your legs in a death grip or if you must hang onto the reins for balance, you have not developed an independent seat or enough balance yet to be able to help your horse learn anything consistent. The only thing your horse will be sure of is that it hurts his back and makes him feel tense all over for you to ride him at the canter or lope. If this is your problem, RUN, don't walk, to get some help with your own balance. Does someone you know have a quiet horse he can help you practice with, while you are schooling your own horse in other exercises from earlier chapters in this book? Do you need to take some lessons from someone who can show you how to feel more confident at the canter or lope than you do now?

One very good exercise to help you is this. Have someone lunge a horse as you are riding it. The horse must be very quiet and dependable, and the handler (the person lungeing the horse) must be knowledgeable as well. You will be working without holding onto the reins, first with stirrups, and then, as you feel more confident, without stirrups. Tie a knot in the reins so the horse doesn't step into them as he works. Let the knotted reins lie on the horse's neck with the knot at his wither, or use a piece of baling twine to tie the knot loosely to the saddle at the withers. The idea is to have the reins out of the rider's way, to have the horse's head free enough to be controlled by the handler's lunge line alone, but, still, to have the reins available should the rider suddenly need to use them.

First, review the feel of the "inside - to- outside" trotting stride beats. Your seat should stay in the saddle, your lower back and legs relaxed. To help keep your balance, you can hold onto the front of the saddle with your hands until you feel secure enough to let go. Don't slouch. Sit up tall. To help you get the feel of the upwards transition to the canter or lope from the sitting trot or the jog, let the handler give the horse the cue to canter as the horse's inside hind leg is coming forward. You will feel your seat going to the outside of the circle. As the handler says, "canter," and you concentrate on following the horse's motion, he will pick up the canter or lope from the trot or jog. Feel the change from the two-beat trot to the three-beat canter. It will take practice over several sessions to get the feel so that you are not left behind at the start and so that you can follow the motion without bouncing.

The motion feels like a three-beat rocking chair gait with the last (third) beat bringing your seat down and forward, as the horse's leading leg strikes the ground. Concentrate on the three-beat feel. Use your hands to pull yourself down into the saddle on that final, third, beat of each stride. Relax your lower back. Soon, you will not need your hands for help. With more practice, you will even be able to work without stirrups.

To come down to trot again, stop the following motion of your lower back and sink your seat straight down, as the handler asks for a downwards transition to trot on the third beat of a canter or lope stride. Relax the next stride and you and the horse should be moving together in a relaxed trot or jog. Finally, try the whole routine — trot to canter, canter a few circles, and canter to trot — while holding the reins and following the horse's motion with your hands, arms, and shoulders as well. When you can do all of this on the lunge line with a helper, you are ready to work on your own at the canter and to apply your own cues or aids to ask the horse for the canter or lope. So, here is the next step. Climb into the saddle on your own horse. Let's ride!

After all the work you have done in using this book, you are well aware by now of the importance of warmup and review. Therefore, be sure you prepare your horse on the lunge line at walk, trot, halt, and canter. Then, warm your horse up under saddle and review his work to this point at the walk, trot, and halt.

Next, you will work the canter or lope, taking the upwards transition from the trot or jog. Here is how.

Begin with your horse at the Western jog or at the sitting English trot on a twenty-foot circle in the corner of the arena. If you are a Western rider, use two hands on the reins, until you and your horse have become better skilled at this new gait. As you trot or jog, concentrate on the feel of your seat bones: inside to outside to inside. One trot stride before you plan to ask for the canter, or perhaps two strides, if your timing and feel are not very precise yet, half-halt for one beat. Then, the next time you feel your seat moving toward the outside of the circle, open your chest, sit straight down, and give a little extra nudge or scoop with that outside side of your seat. If you need to, you can also use your calf muscle of your outside leg a little behind the girth as an added signal, if your horse tends to be a little sluggish. Don't over exaggerate your cues or aids. Just relax with the horse's motion and let things happen naturally and as lightly as possible. As your horse picks up the canter stride, follow his motion. Don't worry about whether he is moving in a Western lope or in an English canter yet. Just get the transition smoothly and the new gait consistently.

Read your horse's reactions to your cues or aids. If he throws his head in the air as you ask and charges off into a fast canter, you asked too harshly. If he pounds off instead at a faster trot, use a little stronger half-halt and then use a light half-halt signal with your inside rein as you use your seat and leg to ask for the canter or lope. Be careful not to tense up and stiffen your body. Follow his movements and relax after you ask. Stay on the circle and bring him back to a calm trot, if he makes a mistake. Trot the whole arena to clear his mind, if you need to. Then, bring him back to the circle and ask for the canter or lope again from a calm trot or jog.

One work of caution here. Some Western riders still persist in the old idea of turning a horse's head to the outside just as they cue for canter or lope. Their reasoning has always been that they are turning the horse to the outside so he has more room to reach forward with his leading front leg and start the lope. That reasoning, however, makes two major mistakes. First, a horse begins his canter or lope from his hind end, not his leading foreleg. Second, he needs to be bent IN the shape of the circle to keep his balance. Turning his nose to the outside throws him off balance and may make him drop his inside or leading shoulder too much, so that he takes the bend stiffly. Besides, why unbalance him at the start and then have to rebalance him to fit the shape of the circle? Why not do things right from the very start?

Once you have your horse traveling consistently at the canter or lope and you feel comfortable and in control, you can practice canter / lope to trot to canter / lope transitions. Remember to half-halt a stride or two before the transition and to work on circles before "going large" around the entire arena on the rail. After your horse is responding well on this task, you can start the process of collection and extension.

HOW DO EXTENSION AND COLLECTION HELP THE RIDER DEVELOP THE CANTER OR THE LOPE?

This work will help you achieve your Western lope or English canter by making your horse even more balanced and ready to learn canter / lope to walk or to halt transitions and halt or walk to canter / lope transitions. Ground poles set twelve feet apart on a circle will get you started on this work. Don't set the poles at six feet apart for work under saddle, until you and your horse are very precise together and your timing is down pat.

Use the same principles you used at the trot to extend or collect. At the canter or lope, just remember you must half-halt on the third beat of the stride. That way, the horse is supporting his weight on the leading leg, his hind feet are off the ground, and he is ready either to round himself more and to collect or to stretch himself out more and to extend. Western lope versus English canter are just a matter of different degrees of extension or collection. Remember, too, that your horse will develop these "gears" on his stride gradually, so don't expect magic results in only one practice session.

One additional little cue you can use to help your horse relax his whole spine and lower his head and neck is this. Hold the reins in two hands. Place your hands low on either side of the withers. As you feel the leading front leg coming forward in the canter/lope stride, gently squeeze the reins very lightly in a downward motion for one beat. Then, go back to the usual motion following the horse's movements. Don't just throw away that light, elastic contact, even if you are a Western rider. Neck reining and those loops in the reins will come after he consistently performs what you want here.

Now, you should feel him flex and relax his lower jaw and reach down and forward with his head and neck. This exercise is especially good to help him stretch out his whole spine for a few minutes before you begin work on collection or as a stretch out after work is done. It also helps when used with a little push from your seat and squeeze with your legs to create extension. It can help your horse to lower his head, if he is carrying it too high. It also helps in relaxing his mind. Just remember. Don't overdo this one for too many minutes or your horse will start getting heavy on his forehand. There has to be a balance between too stretched out and too tensed up, and your half-halts and your judgment and feel are your regulators here.

You can also use this little rein squeezing touch to help a Western or English horse carry his face on a more vertical plain. Use seat and legs to urge him up into your hands. Keep your hands low, and squeeze. Then follow. You will feel him extend, then round a little and give to you, like a coiled spring. Your cues adjust the degree of roundness or "coil."

Last, you can use this little exercise to start feeding your horse more rein, if he is a Western horse. As you squeeze and he gives, let him make the reins a little longer but keep a light touch on them. As the loops get bigger and bigger in the reins, he begins to take lighter and lighter cues from your hands, until he responds on just the weight of the reins alone. When he does this, you can start practicing neck reining with the extension or collection exercises. You can always go back to two hands, if he gets sloppy on you.

What if your horse prefers to gallop rather than to canter? What if he simply will not pay attention? First, ask your self if the "edge" has been worn off of him, that is, if he is still too fresh and needs to be lunged or to play out in the pasture. If he just has a habit of going too fast or of not paying attention, you will have to change his habits gradually. Working circles at various places in the arena and working spiral in and spiral out at the canter or lope can help to solve both of these problems. Just be sure to give your bending cues when the leading leg is down and forward, because that is when the hind legs will be in the air, ready to take their next step to respond to your cue.

After a circle or spiral, go back to working the rail. If the horse starts to rush the canter or lope, circle again. Use half-halts. Slow his rhythm by making your body rhythm slow down a little as you follow his motion. Soon, he will get the idea that you will only allow him to work the rail if he relaxes and keeps the rhythm and shape you want. This rewarding for learning good behavior is much better than beating and yanking on him for rushing. If you yank on him, he will only get more upset and want to run away from your harsh hands. If you make him realize that he will be asked to circle until he calms down, you will help him teach himself that rushing means going nowhere fast in circles.

Circles are also especially good to help a horse who is stiffer going on one lead than on the other, which many horses are. Like people, they tend to be right-sided or left-sided. Working more circles and spirals on your horse's stiff side will help him develop his muscles and learn to balance better, so that he becomes less stiff over time and more flexible. Circles and spirals also help get a distracted horse's attention back on his job and help teach a horse that he can balance his body in a rounder shape.

The last major skill for horse and rider to work on in this chapter is the canter / lope to halt and the halt to canter / lope transition.

HOW DOES THE RIDER TEACH THE HORSE TO DEVELOP SMOOTH CANTER / LOPE TO HALT AND HALT TO CANTER / LOPE TRANSITIONS?

This will be the hardest transition for your horse to learn to do smoothly, because it is so abrupt. He needs a lot of strength and concentration to come down so suddenly and still look quiet and relaxed or to move smoothly upwards from a quiet halt. First, review trot to canter / lope and back to trot transitions as well as collection to get your horse focused. Then, follow this procedure to ask for the halt from the canter or lope.

1.   Make sure he is performing the canter or lope at the right rhythm and in the right shape (frame).

2.   Use two hands on the reins, held low near the withers, and work a twenty-foot circle.

3.   One or two strides before you expect to halt, give your horse a light half-halt as a "wake up call," a message that a change is coming, just as you do before any transition.

4.   One or two strides after the half-halt, feel when the horse's leading leg is down and forward. At that instant, stop the following action of your seat and lower back, close your legs from crotch through calf, and squeeze your fingers down and back on the reins. This should all happen almost simultaneously. Hold for one stride. Then release and follow again.

5.   If your horse only comes to trot or walk or, worse yet, ignores your half-halt cue, then you will have to circle again and ask more strongly and crisply the next time. This stronger cue should get his attention so that he "listens up" and gets the message. Once he gets the idea, you can lighten up on your cue again, making it lighter and lighter to get the same response. Never just keep yanking or pulling on him harshly. You will only make rushing problems worse on a sensitive horse or make a sluggish horse ignore you more. Teach the horse to work lighter and lighter, and he will work happier and smarter, and so will you. Of course, be sure that you sit straight down, when you ask for that halt, because if you lean backward, your seat will be saying "Go!" when you want it to say "Whoa!" Make sure the rushing is not something you are causing by incorrect signals.

Once your horse has halted "square" from the canter or lope, insist that he remain at quiet attention for as many seconds as you decide are necessary, before you ask for the canter / lope from the halt. If he really wants to rush off badly or refuses to stand at a halt, you may have to try this maneuver. Canter him directly into the rail and halt just as his nose nears the rail. He will have to stop or risk bumping his nose on the rail. Of course, the message may come as a bit of a surprise to him. After a few times doing this, though, he should pay better attention and realize he can't ignore your signals. He must come down and stand still at attention. (And you must sit still at the halt too, or you will give him signals to move when you don't mean to.) If you are having way too much trouble with him, though, go back and review his trot-to-halt work first, to get his attention. That's far better than fighting with him over and over at the canter / lope, and it makes for a more positive lesson. If his mind has wandered or his halt is not square, he won't be ready for your next command.

When you are ready to canter / lope, from the square halt, first give your horse a little half-halt to alert him to the coming change (even though he is standing still). Then, give him the usual canter / lope cue. He should move off quietly into the canter / lope. Be careful not to be too harsh, or he will throw his head up and jump forward. Too light a cue may have him just walking off, so learn to read how much of a signal your horse needs. Practice single-handed, if you are a Western rider, after the horse is working well on a two-handed signal. In riding a figure eight at the canter or lope, half-halts are also used a stride or two before the center of the eight, to alert the horse to the coming cue for a change in canter lead. Simple changes (canter/lope to trot/jog to canter/lope) must be smooth and relaxed before flyer changes can be expected or attempted, with the aid of an instructor or knowledgeable grounds person to help you get the timing right.

Now, you should be ready to work the more specialized movements in chapter 7, so on to the next chapter.

DEVELOPING THE HORSE
AND RIDER TEAM'S
PERFORMANCE IN SPECIALIZED
MOVEMENTS

Now that you have completed work with your horse under saddle in walk, trot / jog, canter / lope, halt, upwards and downwards transitions, basic collection, basic extension, and circles and spirals, you are ready to begin work on four specialized movements. These are: the backup, the turn on the forehand, the turn on the haunches, and the sidepass. This chapter will explain how to teach your horse each of these movements under saddle and what particular ground procedures and lunge line work are necessary first to prepare you and your horse.

First, remember all the advice you have been given about preparation and warmup. It is no use jumping into teaching your horse something new unless his mind and body are prepared to learn. Therefore, it is very important that you warm the horse up and that you review things he already knows to prepare him to try the new moves. Let's begin with the backup.

HOW DOES THE RIDER PREPARE THE HORSE FOR THE BACKUP WITH GROUND WORK AND LUNGE LINE WORK?

Begin with the horse wearing a simple halter and lead line. Make sure he is standing quietly and squarely, with all four feet evenly under himself. Stand facing his head and off to the left a little, with your left hand on the lead line about six to eight inches below his chin. In your right hand, hold a dressage whip, pointed at the ground at your side for now. Give a little tug and release, down and back, on the lead line. Use the verbal command, "back." Make sure the horse is paying attention and that he has a chance to think about what you are asking for. Don't rush him, and don't lose his attention.

He will probably do one of three things. First, he may raise his head in resistance. If he does, release the pressure immediately on the line and then try again with a lighter cue. He was probably startled by your command, or he may have been mishandled by someone in the past and was expecting to be yanked around. If you are patient and gentle, he will learn this is no big deal and will give his nose toward his chest. If, instead, he pushes at you with his nose, he either wants to boss you or he thinks this is a game. Either way, with this type of attitude, you have to repeat the verbal command and the tug a little more firmly, until he gets the point. Last, he may just quietly give his chin to his chest, which is what you want him to do.

So, what about getting him to step backward? Once his head is in the correct position, just gently reach toward his front feet, one at a time, and tap his coronet band with the whip. Be careful. Don't make him overreact and strike out or rear. Some horses panic at the whip cue, so, if he is one of these panic button pressers, instead of the whip, try this. With the toe of your boot, gently step on the coronet band of a front hoof, then release. He will pick up the foot and step back with it. As he does, you can tug on the lead line again to see if he will continue stepping back. If not, help him by gently stepping in the same way on the other front foot. Soon, he will get the idea.

As soon as he responds with a couple of steps, stop and praise him. Let him stand quietly for a few seconds. Then, lead him forward for about twenty feet or so. Then, halt square and try the backup again. Soon, he should be moving his front feet and back feet as well. When a horse moves backwards, his feet move diagonally, that is: right front and left hind together, then left front and right hind together, like a backwards trot stride. If he can't get the coordination, shift his weight with a tug on the lead line from one side to another to unbalance him and to make him want to move backwards. You may even have to touch his shoulder with the whip or give him a little poke with the knuckles of your right hand. Just don't overdo your cues.

What if he swings his hindquarters out to one side and doesn't back straight? Work him against a wall first to help him, and don't ask for more than three or four steps at once at first. You will be able to correct this problem. Just don't rush him and make things worse. Also, you can use the dressage whip gently to touch his gaskin or below on his back leg to get him to step straight instead of sideways. Work only for about fifteen minutes per day on this new activity, until he masters it on the lightest cue. Once he has these basics down, he is ready to try the backup on the lunge line with side reins on.

After you have worked him in the normal way on the lunge line with side reins for about fifteen minutes, halt him square. Then, walk up to his head and try the same backup exercise as described above, only this time with the side reins attached. He should get the idea much easier now. As soon as he has completed three or four crisp, straight backup steps, walk him forward and praise him. By this time, he should be ready to try this move under saddle.

HOW DOES THE RIDER WORK THE HORSE INTO THE BACKUP UNDER SADDLE?

Once again, when you try something new under saddle, be sure to use two hands on the reins, even if you are a Western rider. A little farther on here, you will find directions for the one-handed Western backup. First you will teach the horse to back after a walk-to-halt. Then, you will graduate him to backing after trot-to-halt, and finally, after canter / lope-to-halt. Always remember to move your horse forward again after he has completed the backup. Here is how to proceed.

First, as usual, warm the horse and yourself up physically and mentally. Work on walk-to-halt and back to walk transitions for a few minutes. Then, ask for halt and start to teach the backup like this.

At the square halt, keep your hands low on either side of the withers. Lean your body just a tiny bit forward from the hip, just enough to lighten the weight of your seat bones a bit but not enough to stand in your stirrups. Don't show daylight between your seat and the saddle. Squeeze your calf muscles just enough to feel your horse round his back and get ready to take a step forward. Through the reins, almost immediately, you will feel a slight increase in your horse's contact with the bit, because he is getting ready to move his neck forward too, for a step forward. Resist his forward movement with a down and back squeeze of your fingers on the reins. Your horse should lower his head and tuck his chin and back up a step. Go back to neutral with your hands and legs right after he takes that step.

To get the next step back, use leg squeeze into hand squeeze again. Then, release. NEVER use a steady, constant pull, and

NEVER throw your body weight back and try to pull your horse backwards. Since when can you outpull a thousand-pound horse anyway? If you try to do this, your horse will resist and throw his head up high, putting him out of position to respond correctly to your aids. To a judge, he will look unhappy, awkward, and downright unacceptable. You want cooperation, not resistance. Be sure to praise him when he does well and let him walk forward as a reward after the backup.

Try one or two steps at a time and work up to four or five good, straight backward steps, as if he were trotting slowly backwards. Adjust leg and hand cues to help him: a little more leg if he is slow getting started and coming into your hands; a little more hand if he resists giving his jaw and head and wants to walk forward to avoid the backup. Use a wall or rail to help him, if he goes crooked, as you did on the ground work. Drop your leg back on the side needed to prevent his hip from swinging out of line. Also, be sure that you are sitting straight and not making him go crooked by uneven seat bone pressure on his back.

Notice and remember what has just happened. Everything the horse does must come first from "engaging" his hind end's energy. Even in backing up, he must first think forward, so he uses his hind end properly, brings that energy into your hands, then backs off of it. This procedure rounds his spine correctly and makes the backup light and polished. If you can't get him started on that first backward step even after he has relaxed his jaw, try this trick. Think a slow trot backwards. Cue him: right hand to left leg; left hand to right leg. This technique should unfreeze him and get him moving into that first step.

As your horse becomes better at backing up after a walk to halt, try the same exercise after a trot to halt. Coming out of the back this time, encourage your horse to step right back crisply and lightly into trot again. You may have to use a little more leg and seat bone cue, but don't jab at him and don't rush him, or you will lose that calm, smooth, professional, polished performance. If he is a little sluggish, use a light tap with a dressage whip, right behind where your calf muscle rests against his side. Ask with the whip as you ask him with your leg to step forward into trot from backup. It usually only takes a few tries for him to get the message to pay attention and to respond more crisply and lightly to your cue.

When he has mastered the trot to halt to backup to trot, follow the same procedure to work the canter or lope to halt and to backup, then back to canter or lope. Be careful not to rush him or yank on him, or he will throw his head in the air in protest as he takes the halt to lope / canter cue. This action would ruin the calm, polished appearance of his performance. Also, try to get him to respond just to an outside seat bone cue (minus the outside leg cue) with a tiny squeeze pickup on the bridle to get the canter / lope from the backup. Using minimal cues this way, you may help prevent him from swinging his hips out of line and so prevent his looking crooked as he takes the canter departure from the halt. Be careful, too, not to thrust your shoulders forward ahead of his action, because you are trying to give him more momentum. Don't cue the horse with your shoulders. You are sitting on him with your seat, so use your seat bones.

If you are a Western rider, you can begin trying the backup using only one hand on the reins, as soon as your horse feels light and responsive enough. He should take the backup cue on a very light "squeeze back / release" from that single hand. Just tilt your thumb and knuckles back toward your belt buckle by wrist action. Be careful not to pull upwards. Just tilt your hand back using your wrist. The rest of the procedure works the same, so the lighter he becomes in the bridle in two-handed work, the easier he will transfer the idea to your touch from a one-handed signal.

Be sure to reward your horse when he has done well, and, of course, as always, don't expect him to learn everything from walk to canter transitions with the backup in one day. Give him about ten or fifteen minutes work on any new procedure in the middle of your work time with him, after warmup and review and before stretch out and cool down.

Next, you will want to teach the horse two more handy specialized moves, which will put that extra polish and maneuverability on him in the show ring and out on the trail as well. These are the turn on the haunches and the turn on the forehand. Both of these moves can be started through the proper lessons on the ground, working the horse in a halter and lead and using a dressage whip.

HOW DOES THE RIDER BEGIN THE TURN ON THE HAUNCHES FROM THE GROUND?

In this move, the horse keeps his haunches in place and moves only his forehand, stepping with his front feet to either the right or to the left. This movement is begun from a quiet, square halt, so be sure the horse is paying attention and is prepared to stand quietly. Halt the horse with his right side parallel to a wall or rail. Leave yourself enough room to stand just in front of him but off to his right side a little. Stand facing him with the lead line in your right hand, about eight to ten inches from his chin and under it. At your side, in your left hand, hold a dressage whip.

Be sure he is standing square and that his focus is on you. If he is looking around, tug on the lead line lightly to get his attention. Next, give a little tug on the line down and out to his left (to your right, because you are facing him, remember?) He should take a step or two out to his left, sideways, with his front feet only. If he doesn't move, tap gently on his right shoulder with the tip of the dressage whip as you give the tugging cue on the lead line. He should get the idea. Be careful not to let him step into a backup. If he does this, stop him, lead him forward, square halt him again, and start over. He must think "over," not "back."

If he tries to swing his hips to the right as his front end goes left, the wall or rail will stop him. Don't let him walk over you either. Halt him, square his halt up, and try again. All you need for now is that he get the basic idea that he can take one or two or even three steps over with his front legs (forehand) independent of his hind legs (haunches). Work on this exercise for ten or fifteen minutes or so, six or seven minutes on each side. (To ask him to go to the right with his forehand, just reverse the positions: wall or rail on his left; you standing at his left.)

Once the horse gets the idea working in basic halter and lead, you can also ask him to perform the same maneuver in side reins. This will help him keep his frame together easier as he steps sideways. The next step, of course, is to try the same thing under saddle. This time, your seat, legs, and hands will help your horse get the idea of how to perform.

HOW DOES THE RIDER USE HIS SEAT, LEGS, AND HANDS TO TEACH THE HORSE THE TURN ON THE HAUNCHES FROM THE SADDLE?

Once the horse has been warmed up and is paying attention, work some small circles and spirals on him at the walk and trot to get him focused. Then, come to a square halt with his outside side parallel to one rail or wall. Your horse should be standing at attention. Western riders should be using two hands on the reins at this point.

Let's suppose the rail is on your left and you want to start a turn on the haunches to the right. You will follow four basic steps. First, use a little squeeze with your calf muscles to make your horse think he will be asked to move forward. He must think "forward" to get his hind end in gear, remember? Also, you need that hind end energy to come into your hands. You should feel a slight increase in your horse's bit contact with the bridle. Now, he is ready to move.

Okay, second, you need to get him to lighten his forehand and transfer his front end weight back to his haunches, so he can step sideways lightly with his front feet. What? But you just asked him to engage his hind quarters and get ready to send that energy into your hands. Yes, but that was in order to get his hind end under him and ready to work, ready to support his weight. Otherwise, he would be "strung out behind" and he would have too much weight on his front end (forehand) once you did ask him to move his front feet in a sideways step. So, how do you get him to lighten his forehand? Use a little half-halt. Now you are ready for step three and so is his hind end.

In step three, pretend you are going to make a very tight circle: inside leg squeeze into outside supporting hand; outside leg back and keeping the horse's hip in the shape of the circle (so the hip won't swing wide to the left when you will ask the horse to move his forehand to the right.) Having a wall or rail on the horse's left side also helps keep his hip in place for now. Later, you should practice this movement at various spots in the arena, after he has gotten the idea of moving his forehand while keeping his haunches in place.

Finally, for step four, you will make the actual move, teaching the horse a little at a time over several days or even weeks. Here is what to do. Your horse needs to step to the right with his front legs while keeping his hind legs in place, right? Okay, when you support with that outside (the left here) hand and outside leg, squeeze down and back toward your right hip a little with your outside hand and add a tiny bit more weight to your inside (right here) seat bone. This action transfers his weight to what will become his pivot foot, the inside hind. Use a squeeze - release cue and use your inside (right) rein to prevent forward motion and to encourage the horse to take a step at a time to the right with his front feet. Don't let him turn his nose to the outside. If he tries to avoid your command and backs up, use a little leg pressure to prevent him from letting his energy escape your aids. The reaction should be: squeeze - step - release - squeeze - step - release. He should cross over in front. After two or three steps, reverse your cues to return the horse to a straight forward position. Ask him to stand quietly for a moment or two. Then, walk him calmly forward. Pat and praise him. Practice doing this on the other side as well, reversing the inside and outside now, of course.

Over a few weeks, you will see him get the idea better and

learn to set his inside hind leg as a pivot foot to step around. When he has learned to do a 180 degree turn and to stand quietly afterwards, waiting for the cue to walk on forward, he is ready for Western riders to try this one-handed. Trying one-handed too soon may cause him to turn his nose to the outside of the turn and to drop his inside shoulder, a badly balanced picture to say the least. If you feel you are forcing him with a neck rein cue, so that he starts to resist or lays on your hands and tips his nose toward an incorrect position, go back to two hands. A neck rein turn must be done smoothly, without resistance. It represents a polished move. If the basics aren't there, the polish will most certainly not be there either.

Another exercise to help your horse become more fluid in the turn on the haunches, once he has the basic idea, is to work into the turn on the haunches from a spiral down into a smaller and smaller circle. Just before asking for the turn on the haunches, be sure to half-halt, but don't stop his motion to a complete halt. He should begin to learn that he can change drection 180 degrees this way, while still keeping a smooth motion flowing forward from behind. Now, when you want to change directions in the show ring at the walk, your horse will look smooth and polished and won't need to make a huge circle to make the change.

The next manuever to teach your horse is the turn on the forehand. For this movement, you will proceed in much the same fashion: lead line and halter preparation; side rein improvement in movements; polished performance under saddle.

HOW DOES THE RIDER TEACH THE HORSE THE TURN ON THE FOREHAND FROM THE GROUND?

Begin with the horse in the halter and lead. This time, pick a place in the center of the arena with no rail for him to bump into, because you want his forehand to be still while his hind legs step freely around this forehand. To work the turn on the forehand going to the left, stand on the horse's right side. To work the turn going to the right, stand on the horse's left side.

Suppose you wish to begin by teaching the horse to move his haunches to his left. Grasp the lead a few inches from the halter with your right hand, as you stand facing your horse from the front and a little off to his right side. In your left hand, hold a dressage whip at your side. Be sure the horse is standing quietly square. Get his attention with a little tug on the line. Then, reach over gently with your dressage whip and tap him on the gaskin of his right rear leg. At the same time that you tap his hind leg, resist his forward movement with your right hand on the lead line. Thus, his only option will be to step sideways away from your whip. Be careful not to tug too hard on the lead line, or your horse may decide that you meant to ask him for a crooked back-up. He may step sideways and back at the same time, not what you want. You will have to adjust your cues to fit your horse's response.

Ask him to take one relaxed step at a time. Don't get after him so much that he panics and walks all over you or rushes back-wards away from you. If he is sluggish, you may have to tap a lit-tle more firmly, but remember, he must think of this in a relaxed but attentive way. Ask him to take no more than three steps at a time. Then, quietly shift to the other side of him, and ask him to step back into his original position. Work both sides of the horse, asking him to step sideways with his hind legs only, while keep-ing his forehand in place. If he gives you a lot of trouble about walking over you instead of stepping sideways, you may have to resort to facing him into a wall or rail, so that he cannot go for-ward at all. Then, you can graduate him to working in the center of the arena, once he has the general idea of what you would like him to do.

Next, of course, once you have worked this movement with the lead line, you can do the same thing in side reins to polish the move a little. Finally, you will ask him to develop this movement under saddle.

HOW DOES THE RIDER TEACH THE TURN ON THE FOREHAND FROM THE SADDLE?

After a warmup of circles and spirals, this movement begins again with the quiet, square halt. Western riders use two hands until your horse has gotten the basic idea. Let's assume that you would like to teach your horse to keep his forehand still while stepping to the left with his hind legs or haunches. First, use your seat and calf muscles to nudge your horse very gently, so you can feel his hindquarter energy come into your hands through the reins. Resist his forward motion with a squeeze on the reins held low, near his withers. The left rein squeeze should be back while the right rein squeeze should be to the left and back, transferring energy to the left hind leg. At the same time, let just a touch more weight come into your left seat bone, as you drop your right leg behind the girth and squeeze your calf muscle on that leg to urge your horse to step to the left with his haunches. The action should be: squeeze - step - release; squeeze - step - release. Never use a steady pull or a steady, unyielding leg pressure.

If your horse is sluggish, use a dressage whip behind your right leg to tap him into stepping over to the left. If he is trying to walk forward through your hands, face him into a wall or rail, until he gets the idea that he cannot play the "walk away from the job" game. If he tries to back up, urge him to walk forward, halt him squarely again, and try again. Try just one step, then gradually work to doing two steps, and finally to doing three or four steps to the left. After several weeks of schooling, the horse should be able to set his inside front leg as a pivot foot and turn 180 degrees as his haunches step around his forehand. Always remember to ask the horse to step back into his original halt position each time you try this move by reversing your aids. Then, ask him to walk forward and pat and praise him.

To turn to the right, use right rein back, left rein back and toward the right hip, more weight in right seat bone, and left leg behind the girth to squeeze the horse's hips to the right. Once the horse has the idea of working smoothly in both directions, Western riders may replace the two-handed cues with the neck rein, applied back and toward the left hip to move left and back and to the right hip to move right.

Last, you will teach the horse the sidepass and the related leg yield, both lateral moves in which the forehand and haunches both move sideways at the same time, a handy skill for your horse to have available both on the trail and in the show ring.

HOW DOES THE RIDER PREPARE THE HORSE FOR THE SIDEPASS AND THE LEG YIELD WITH GROUND WORK?

Begin, once again, working the horse from the ground in a halter and lead line out in the center of the arena. Let's say that you wish to ask your horse to step to the right and forward at the same time. This action will mean that he will need to walk forward and sideways at the same time. He will begin by crossing the "stepping" left leg over in front of the "stationary" right leg, both front and hind. He should not knock into his right leg with his left leg or step on himself awkwardly, like a new dancer fumbling through his first dance steps. You want him to move fluidly and gracefully. Also, you shouldn't expect him to step sideways a great deal in his first few lessons. He may cross over only a little at first. This is a new idea for him, remember, this going forward and sideways at the same time. So, here's how to show him what's up.

If he will be moving right, you will be standing on his left, with your left hand on his lead line about six or eight inches from his chin and under it. You should be facing his shoulder and holding a dressage whip in your right hand at your side. He should be standing at a quiet, square halt. Okay, let's get him started.

Extend your left arm out to his right, as if you were asking him to walk on away from you. At the same time, reach up with your dressage whip and tap him gently on his barrel, just about where your left leg would rest if you were in the saddle. As he starts to move, go with him. You will be walking backwards and to his right as he walks forward and to his right. Keep an eye on his legs and don't rush him. Use gentle tugs on the lead line and gentle taps with the dressage whip to keep his rhythm even and steady. Tug on the lead line and tap with the whip just as his inside hind leg is coming forward. You might need to tap him on his gaskin to ensure that his hind end keeps up with his front end, and you may have to resist his front end movement a little, if he's the type who is slow about getting his hind end in gear. If his forehand always seems to get ahead of his hind end, try asking him with the dressage whip a moment before you use your hand on the lead line for the first step. That way, he will think more about starting the action from his hind end first, as he should anyway.

After he has taken a few walking steps forward and sideways like this, halt him, and pat and praise him. Then, lead him off at a normal walk for a few strides. Then, stop him square and start the move over again. Do this five or six times on each side of him the first time you try this. After a few days, or even a week, when he has gotten the idea that he can go forward and sideways smoothly and quietly, you can add the side reins arrangement, to help him keep his frame together better. Only after all of this preparation has been done, should the horse be asked to begin walking under saddle in this maneuver.

HOW DOES THE RIDER TEACH THE HORSE THE SIDE-PASS AND THE LEG YIELD FROM THE SADDLE?

First, you will need to warm your horse up by working the spiral in and the spiral out at the walk. As preparation for the sidepass, he will learn to work the leg yield. In this move, he is bent for a circle, but you send him off of the circle on a tangent. In other words, if he is to leg yield to the left, you will warm him up with a spiral in and out to the right. On the last circle of the spiral out, you will ask him to keep his spine bent to the circle, but now he will go off the circle, forward and sideways to the left, as he did in the ground work you did with him earlier. Sounds simple, but how do you get him to do this?

The answer lies in using your seat bones, legs, and hands correctly. Western riders use two hands for now. You already know how to ask your horse for the spiral in and the spiral out. Remember, when you ask for the spiral out, you change your seat bones so that you add a little weight to your outside seat bone. Your horse wants to come up under this weight to feel even and balanced again. Your inside leg and seat bone cue the horse to step forward and sideways to the outside of the circle just as his inside hind leg is coming forward. Your outside leg and outside hand will receive the energy of this sideways movement. If your horse wants instead to lead with his outside shoulder and let his hind end drag behind the sideways movement, resist (really support) his outside shoulder with a little pressure from your outside leg at the girth and a little squeeze back with your outside hand. This action will prevent his shoulder from getting ahead of his hips. If he wants to move only forward and not sideways at all, resist his forward motion with a squeeze of both hands in rhythm with his inside hind leg movement. After he has given you two or three steps of forwards and sideways, allow him to walk on normally, and pat and praise him. Over a couple of weeks, you will notice that he moves more and more easily into this action of yielding sideways to your leg as he comes out of the spiral out and that he will give you more and more steps, until he may even be able to travel thirty or forty feet performing this move. Don't rush him and don't get angry with him. Keep your squeezes in rhythm with his inside leg movement, as always. If you need to tap with a dressage whip behind your inside leg, use it as his inside leg is coming forward.

The next step, of course, is to ask him to change that leg yield into a full sidepass. How? Simply resist his forward motion more and insist more on sideways motion. All you are doing is slowly, that is, gradually over several weeks, asking him to eliminate the forward part of the motion while still maintaining the sideways motion. Before long, you will be able to ask him to step directly sideways after the spiral out. Eventually, you will be able to ask him to step sideways from the square halt, without the preparation of the spiral out exercise beforehand. All of this takes time, so don't expect too much too fast, or you will mix him up and ruin his attitude. Then you will have problems to fix. Why create problems, when patience, perception, planning, and persistence will give you the movement you want and a happy horse besides?

Developing this movement gradually as described above teaches the horse to think to move forward from behind, so he stays light on his forehand and looks graceful to a judge in the show ring. If you need to move him sideways off the rail and back on again in a performance class or if you need to straighten him up while standing in a lineup waiting for the judge's decision on a class, all you will need to do is to give him subtle sideways cues and his "sideways gears" will step him lightly just where you want him to be.

If you are a Western rider, wait until your horse has mastered the full sidepass two-handed, before you change to one-handed work, so that both you and your horse have a firm foundation in the movement. When you begin to use one-handed reining, that is neck reining, remember to keep your hand low in front of the saddle horn, but not too low. A hand held below his withers will prevent you from asking for sideways movement of his forehand. Also, do not place your hand any further up on the horse's neck than his crest or he may raise his head in resistance. Remember to use the hinge action of your wrist. Also, remember that the horse's energy is coming from his inside hind leg into your outside rein, so that neck rein on the outside must stay in contact with his neck to receive the energy from his inside hind leg. That outside rein is providing resistance and support.

With all of these specialized movements in place as part of your horse's repertoire of skills, you are not ready to put the final polish on you and your horse as a performance team. Onward to chapter eight.

PUTTING THE PIECES TOGETHER:
Developing Stamina and a Fluid, Balanced Performance Team

Throughout this book, you and your horse have worked on perfecting individual gaits, transitions, and specialized movements. You planned carefully and worked patiently, focusing each lesson on the particular goal you had in mind. Your lessons or schooling sessions with your horse developed you and your horse, one skill at a time, like an artful mason crafts a foundation, building block by building block.

The time has come to put the final polish on all of your hard work. Your goals now will be to increase stamina and to give this performance team, you and your horse, that final graceful touch of balance and fluid movement that says, "I am the competitor to watch," to the judge in the show ring.

Whether you are an English or a Western rider, you and your horse must have sufficient stamina to avoid becoming winded and tired half way through a performance class. If you plan to show all day, say in five or six classes, both you and your horse must be sufficiently fit to endure a long day of competition, especially in hot weather. By now, you have noticed that working your horse correctly four or five days each week under saddle, anywhere from forty-five minutes to sixty minutes, including lunge line warm up, has increased fitness levels for both of you. What's more, your skill has grown too, and you are feeling a lot more confident about competing in the show ring. Your horse's attention span has increased as well, for he has learned mental discipline as well as physical conditioning, and so have you.

Despite all of these positive results, however, both of you, as competitors, need to have that extra edge to be ready to compete, for a couple of reasons. First, just the jangled nerves of show day can cause both you and your horse to look less than your best. Second, working five or six classes in one day, with each class running fifteen to twenty minutes, can exhaust a horse and rider whose work sessions at home last only an hour a day. Relaxing between show classes at the trailer in the shade may give some relief, but both you and your horse will need to be prepared for stress beyond your daily routine.

HOW DOES THE RIDER BUILD STAMINA IN BOTH HIM-SELF / HERSELF AND THE HORSE?

In the first place, you would never plan to show your horse in five or six classes all in one day or to take him away from home to a one- or two-day show, if you and your horse were new to show-ing. You would start your show season by attending a show close to home and by showing in only one or two classes. You can add to the number of classes, the distance in travel time, and the length of your stay at a show by planning your show season carefully with breaks for your horse and yourself. You don't want to be running off to a show every weekend. Also, if a particularly long show is on your schedule, make sure you arrive a day early to settle your horse in at the show grounds' overnight stabling facilities.

Due to the stress of competition, you may find that your horse will need an extra supply of electrolytes. These are miner-als — potassium, sodium, chloride — which are needed by your horse's body to aid nerve impulses and muscle contraction. Your horse loses these minerals through his sweat, so if he must per-form for longer periods under more stress, he may lose more than he would by just being worked at home. Without a suffi-cient supply of these minerals, he runs the risk of tying up, suf-fering painful and dangerous spasms of the large muscles and even risking kidney failure in severe cases. This type of danger is more common in hot weather, when your horse sweats away minerals and salt from his system even more quickly. What should you do to protect your horse? Ask your veterinarian for a supply of electrolytes and for directions in using them correctly.

If you do use electrolytes, they will be added to your horse's water. Be sure also, however, to supply him with a second bucket of water, free of the electrolyte mixture. Why? Horses have an instinct for when their bodies need electrolytes and seem to know when to drink the electrolyte water. If you do not provide your horse with that second bucket of plain, clean, electrolyte-free water, he may not drink enough water at all, and so could become dangerously dehydrated. He doesn't need electrolytes all the time, but he does need access to fresh, clean water all the time (except, as you know, when he is so hot that he must be cooled down before drinking).

Okay, what about increasing his work time under saddle at

home, so that you and he can eventually endure those long showing days of five and six classes in a day's showing? Gradually, you can increase your work time from one hour to one and one-half hours. You can work your horse for one hour in the morning and a second time in the evening, working up to a total of two hours. You can work a one hour session in the ring for schooling and then allot a second session to trail riding, where you trot uphill and canter level one-half to one-mile stretches.

During your schooling sessions in the ring, you can increase the number of laps around the ring which you take at a given gait. Watch to see when your horse begins to blow, his nostrils flaring, his sides blowing in and out. Give him a walking break, not a standing still one. Standing still can cause tight muscles. Then, when he has caught his breath in three to five minutes, go back to work. Try to ask for an additional one-half lap or one lap around the ring before you let him walk and blow on the next day's lesson. Watch his respiration rate, degree of sweat, and spring of gait. Eventing riders will tell you that they even take their horses' pulse to check his physical condition. Have your veterinarian show you how to do this and also ask your vet to explain how to determine and to evaluate your horse's recovery time in pulse and respiration. While you are talking to your vet, ask him to explain the signs of typing up, colic, dehydration, and heat exhaustion in a horse, if you are not familiar with what to watch for, what to do about these problems, and how to prevent them. Waiting until you are in strange territory at a show is no time to take emergency lessons in handling such potentially life-threatening health problems. This is definitely a case where knowledge is power, power to prevent disaster.

Last, don't forget to give your own fitness for competition the same care you have given to your horse. As you increase the number of laps around the ring your horse will travel, you yourself should be increasing your fitness to ride him for longer and longer periods of time. Working without stirrups for increasingly longer periods of time is one way to strengthen your legs and improve your balance. Use your cross-training routines with weights and / aerobic exercise, as mentioned earlier in this book, to enhance your own overall fitness level. Check with your own doctor about precautions you should take to avoid dehydration and heat exhaustion on those busy, hot show days. Take care to be sure you eat, drink, and rest sufficiently. You and your horse are equally important parts of your performance team. Don't neglect yourself.

Next, as you work through your schooling sessions with your horse, you will also now be putting the finishing touches on your performance together. So, here is the next obvious question:

HOW DOES THE RIDER ACHIEVE THAT FINAL, GRACE-FUL TOUCH OF BALANCE AND FLUID MOVEMENT WITH HIS HORSE?

The answer to this question lies in attention to detail, timing, imaging, and calm, intelligent practice. For this polish, rely on your own judgment plus the eye of an experienced ground person, who can point out little things you or your horse might be doing that you weren't even aware of.

First, take mental inventory of your position in the saddle and your attitude about the job at hand. Talk over any problems you think you may be having with your ground person, and ask him or her to take note of what you are doing and how effective you are in changing what may be incorrect. Picture yourself as a competent rider who can do the job, and pay special attention to erasing the last remains of any old habits that you have been working to rid yourself of as a rider. Are you still causing your horse to drop his inside shoulder around corners, because you let your inside seat bone get too heavy? Are you forgetting to half-halt before corners and gait changes and halts? Are your half-halts too harsh or too light? Are you using your hands first instead of seat, legs, hands? Does your leg creep out of position? Do you allow yourself to fall too far onto your crotch or too far back onto the cantle of the saddle, like a "roly-poly" doll ready to topple backwards or forwards? If so, work on getting your seat and lower back to follow the horse more. Are your shoulders over your hips and your hips and heels in vertical alignment? Are your hands low and subtly following the horse's motion, even through to your shoulders? Are you looking where you are going and planning your moves? Is your timing in rhythm with the horse's inside hind leg movements? Are you working smoothly and naturally, or are you trying so hard that your moves appear rushed and jerky? Do you breathe deeply and naturally, letting your breathing rhythm connect with the horse's rhythm? Do you look confident and happy to be on your horse, or are you frowning and nervous or angry or frustrated? Make a list, with the aid of your ground person, of the last little rough spots that you want to get rid of in your own performance. Then, turn to what your horse's performance needs in polish.

Your horse's attitude and physical readiness must go hand in hand. If his attention is still wandering at a certain gait, use your ground person to help you figure out why? Are there other horses in a nearby field he'd rather play with? Is he in the habit of rushing into the canter from the trot, because he is "canter happy"? Does he need more work on transitions and more circles and spirals to get him focused? Or are you just missing the signs that he is about to rush with you, allowing him to get two jumps ahead of you before you make a correction? Is he sluggish or sour from too much ring work and in need of a trail ride to refresh his mind and his outlook on his work, as well as to give his muscles a different kind of workout? Is he ignoring your leg and hand cues or overreacting to them? Should you be lighter or firmer and crisper? You are the one who must affect the change. You are the leader who shows the horse the way to success.

What about your horse's skill in performing? Does he need more circles to get him to bend on his stiff side? Are his corners balanced? Does he need some leg yielding practice at the walk, trot, and canter down the rail, so that you can place him anywhere you wish as he goes? You might need to avoid a collision in the show ring with another rider or need to position yourself in a spot where the judge will see you more clearly. Will he extend or collect any of his gaits on your command and stay collected or extended until you ask for a change? Does he throw his head a little on upwards or downwards transitions? Why? His habit or your hands being too harsh? Or your leg and seat cues being too abrupt? Are his halts square and quiet, or does he need to get his haunches under him more and then practice the discipline of standing quietly at the halt, waiting for your next command? Is his backup smooth or still choppy and crooked? Can you move his forehand and haunches separately and subtly to position him any way you may need to?

Work calmly and intelligently with your ground person, until you have solved any problems your horse may still be having. Analyze why and how they happen and how you may be causing them to happen. Check to see how effective your corrections are. Go back to earlier chapters in this book and reread directions for any moves that may still be a problem for you and your horse. When you are finally satisfied with all of the pieces of your performance, ask your ground person to call out commands to you at random to change gaits, change direction, halt, backup, etc. See if you and your horse can perform on command with calm, focused purpose. Now you are ready to turn to chapter nine and to explore just exactly what the judge will be looking for in each of the show ring classes discussed in this book.

PRACTICING FOR THE SHOW RING AT HOME:
What the Judge will expect in:
Western Pleasure, Hunter Under saddle, Western Horsemanship,
and Hunt Seat Equitation

Before you enter any show ring class, you must know what movements or routines the judge will expect you and your horse to perform in that type of class, how they should be done, and what general rules of etiquette you must follow. No matter how well your horse performs for you at home, if you are not informed about particular procedures and performance requirements, you will be in for a sudden surprise the day you set foot in that show ring. The last thing you want to do is find yourself confused and embarrassed when you want to make a good impression. So, let's look at each of the classes mentioned in this chapter's title, one by one, step by step.

WHAT WILL THE JUDGE BE LOOKING FOR IN WESTERN PLEASURE IN HORSE AND RIDER?

Let's take the class routine from beginning to end. Riders walk their horses into the show ring at the entrance gate and turn to the right, thus traveling around the rail going to the left. As each rider enters one at a time, the judge will look at him or her and his mount, sizing them up. At the very start, you and your horse want to make a good impression, so you should be prepared and "with it" the second you enter that arena, head up and smiling confidently.

Although the horse in a pleasure class is judged more than the rider, a bad rider can ruin even a good horse's performance, so be on the alert to help your horse perform at his best. The judge will be looking for a slow, even, relaxed, soft, four-beat walk. He will also check to see that the horse is traveling on a loose, lightly held rein. The horse should be neither drooping sloppily and heavily on his forehand like a ton of bricks nor wound up tense and tight like a bomb ready to go off. The horse's ears should be just about level with his withers, not lower, his ears should be pointing ahead with interest in his job, and the plain of his face should be on or nearly on the vertical, not cranked back behind the vertical. His tail should lay calm and quiet, not twitching in annoyance. Essentially, the horse and rider should make the appearance of a comfortable team that is pleasing to watch. As you travel around the ring, make sure that your corners are deep and round and that you stay straight on the rail at all gaits. Also, try to stay at least two horse lengths behind the horse in front of you.

After all contestants have entered the ring, the judge will determine how long he or she wishes to observe the class at the walk. All contestants will remain at the walk until asked to jog. At the cue to jog, it is wise for each contestant to give the rider in front of him a moment to make the upwards transition to the jog. No rider wants to rush into this move and look like he is in the ring to play bumper cars with the rider ahead of him. However, no contestant wants to wait so long to make the transition that he gives the judge the impression that he cannot get his mount to change gait on cue.

You, as the rider, must remain alert to determine the best moment to make your move, while keeping your horse's attention focused on you. You don't want your horse to surprise you by jogging off before you are ready and leaving you a beat behind in the saddle. If your horse wants to rush, you should know this about his personality by now and should be planning ahead with tiny vibrations on the reins to keep his attention and little, invisible half-halts to keep his mind on the gait you want him to maintain until you ask for a change. If he is sluggish, you should be invisibly encouraging him by swinging your seat bones a little more in rhythm with his hip movement, not so much that the judge could notice that you are driving your horse forward, though. Tiny squeezes with your calf muscles can also help here.

At the jog, the horse should move collected, slow, and smooth in a definite two-beat cadence. He should maintain the same relaxed look he had at the walk. When he makes the upwards transition, he should not throw his head or rush off. Neither should he require obvious urgings from his rider, whose aids should be very subtle. He will work on a loose rein with light contact, as he did at the walk.

Usually horse and rider are asked to make the downward transition to the walk again before they are asked to pick up the lope. The downward transition from the jog to the walk should be smooth, with the rider keeping the same light contact on the bridle, with loose reins. Obvious jerking backwards with the hands will count against the performance, for the horse will look as though he does not want to make the downward transition. The rider should be careful to sink his seat straight down into the walk, so that his upper body doesn't fall forward out of the horse's center of gravity, as the downward transition is made. The wise thing to do, of course, is to watch the contestant in front of you and to give your horse a little, invisible half-halt a stride or two before that downward transition, to prepare the both of you for the change in gait.

Next comes the departure into the lope from the walk. Again, the horse should stay collected and relaxed and should strike off in an even, three-beat rhythm. He should not break into the trot before he begins to lope, and he should not throw his head at the upward transition and rush off. His lope should be slow and cohesive but should never be so slow that it degenerates into a four-beat gait, that is cantering in front and trotting behind. Of course, the horse must strike off at the start on the correct lead and should be working on a loose rein with a light contact and minimal corrections on your part to keep him consistent. Even if your horse's natural collected lope may be a little faster than another horse's, your horse may place ahead of that slower horse, if the slower horse's lope has broken down into a four-beat gait.

When the judge has decided he has seen what he needs to see from the contestants at the lope, riders will be asked to make the transition from the lope to the walk. Again, the judge will be looking for a smooth, relaxed downward transition without a lot of pulling on the reins. The horse should maintain the low, relaxed frame and should sink down from his hindquarters into the walk without falling on his forehand. He should walk on smoothly and quietly, not tossing his head or chewing at the bit, eager to begin to lope again. You, as an alert contestant, will, of course, give your horse that opportunity to look his best by giving him the necessary half-halt before you expect the transition to walk, sinking your seat, and staying out of his mouth.

At the walk again, now, riders will be asked to turn or pivot 180 degrees and work the same class routine the opposite way around the arena. Here's where that work in turning on the haunches that you did at home will come in handy for polish and style.

Working the rail in the opposite direction, the horse should show the same consistency and balance at all gaits. In the lope, he should take the correct lead as easily as he did in the other direction. The horse and rider may be asked to perform a halt from the lope. The halt should be square and quiet, with the downward transition made with the same grace as other transitions, despite the extreme of halting from the faster gait. The horse should sink his hindquarters and be willing to stand quietly at the halt until asked to move on.

At this point, rail work is complete. Riders will be asked to come to the center of the arena and line up facing the judge's stand, one rider beside the other. Each rider will then be asked individually to back his horse four or five steps and walk him forward again to halt before the judge. You should keep your eyes on the judge and make sure your horse is at attention when your turn comes to perform. The judge will be looking for a straight, relaxed backup, with the horse giving his jaw and stepping back lightly and willingly without chewing on the bit or tossing his head or going crooked with his hindquarters.

When the last contestant has backed his mount, the class then waits to be pinned. During the time the judge is making his final decision, it is both polite and wise to sit quietly at attention. Ribbon winners are usually called to come forward to claim a ribbon from lowest place up through the blue, which is called last. If you receive a ribbon, accept it gracefully with thanks. All riders should exit the arena promptly, pleasantly, and in a dignified manner, whether or not they are ribbon winners.

Now, how about the next class?

WHAT WILL THE JUDGE BE LOOKING FOR IN HUNTER UNDER SADDLE IN HORSE AND RIDER?

Once again, riders will enter the arena at a walk and turn to the right. The horse should be working on direct contact, with the bridle rein forming a straight line this time from the rider's elbow through to the corner of the horse's mouth. The walk should be slow (though not as slow as the Western Pleasure walk), controlled, business-like, and four-beat. The horse's ears should be level with his withers, with his face on a vertical plain or slightly ahead of the vertical. Rider and horse should have a calm, confident appearance. In the walk, rather than showing collection, the horse's legs should sweep out gracefully from the shoulders and hips and reach flatly to the ground in a style horsemen call a "daisy-cutter walk." Although the walk here has more energy than the Western Pleasure walk, excessive speed is penalized, for this would indicate that the horse is rushing forward.

The trot, too, has more energy and extension than the Western Pleasure trot and should be floating, flat, and long, but still controlled and not rushed. A definite two-beat gait is expected, and downward transitions to walk must be as smooth as they are in Western Pleasure, even though that additional energy and extension are present in the horse's stride. The judge will indicate the call for gait changes, as in the Western Pleasure class.

When the class is asked to depart from the trot into the canter, the canter will be controlled, round, and smooth but not as collected and slow as the Western Pleasure lope. There will be more energy and extension in this performance than in the Western Pleasure movement. At the departure, of course, the judge is watching the horse for errors such as head tossing, grabbing the bit, and charging off. The judge will also take off points for a horse who continues in the trot too long before making the upwards transition, hammering along at a bone-jarring trot ,and finally falling on his forehand into a rushed canter. The canter will be a true three-beat gait, and the rider should have control and contact through the bridle at all times. Correct leads at the canter, of course, are just as important as they are in the Western Pleasure class.

After the class has worked in one direction, the judge will ask for the reversal with work on the rail in the opposite direction. The judge will be looking for consistency in both directions as well as balance. Points will be lost for a horse who travels faster or more stiffly in one diretion than the other. The halt from the canter should have the same calm consistency as the halt in the Western Pleasure class, even though the horse is now traveling with more energy and extension.

Procedures in the lineup at the center of the arena, where the backup is required, are similar to the routine in Western Pleasure, except, of course, that the English rider will be backing his horse up using two hands.

Okay, now let's look at the classes which judge the rider's control of the horse over the horse's performance.

WHAT WILL THE JUDGE BE LOOKING FOR IN WESTERN HORSEMAN-SHIP AND HUNT SEAT EQUITATION?

Both of these classes begin with a lineup at one end of the arena. Each exhibitor will be called to work an individual pattern within a thirty-second time limit. The pattern will be judged on how well the pattern is negotiated, on the rider's seat and posture, and on how well the rider maintains the horse's smoothness and consistency of gait. Patterns will be posted at the show grounds at least an hour or more (usually in the morning) before a class, so that contestants may review what will be expected of them. Horses are ridden in a more collected manner for these classes with more "on the bit" contact than in Western Pleasure or Hunter Under Saddle. Western riders will work on a shorter rein than in a pleasure class.

In both Western and English classes here, the rider's position should show that his ear, hip, elbow, and heel are in an imaginary vertical line and that he is in harmony with his horse's center of gravity, at whichever gait he may be riding. His heels should rest lower than his toes, with either the ball of the foot resting on the stirrup or with the stirrup shoved "home" to the heel of the boot. (The ball of the foot position is preferable, as it provides more flexibility for the rider.) In Western classes, the rein hand should be within four inches of the saddle horn, thumb up. In English classes, the hands should be "thumbs up" with the hands tilted thirty degrees in toward each other. The angle from the rider's elbows to the corners of the horse's mouth should be at 45 degrees. In Western classes, the rider sits straight at all gaits, changing his position only very slightly to maintain harmony with his horse's center of gravity. In English classes, the rider sits straight for the walk and sitting trot , but his upper body is inclined slightly forward from the hip for the posting trot, in harmony with the horse's center of gravity change. (There will be more forward energy in the posting trot than in the Western jog.) In English classes, the rider's canter position will be slightly ahead of the walk position but not as forward as the posting trot position, as the rider does not rise to the canter as he does to the trot. Rising at the canter shows an inability to maintain a fluid, following seat at this gait.

Contestants may be asked to perform a number of movements, designed into the pattern for the day's class. Patterns should be maneuvered smoothly and cleanly, whatever is called upon in whatever order. Riders may be asked to perform a serpentine, a flying or simple lead change, and / or a figure eight. All types of transitions may be called for from any gait to any other gait. English riders may be asked to perform sitting and / or posting trot. English riders may also be asked to perform the hand gallop. Turn on the haunches may be required at 90, 180, 270, or 360 degrees. A backup and a dismount / mount may also be required.

When all exhibitors have executed the required pattern, riders will be asked to work on the rail as a rail class, working movements at the discretion of the judge. Gaits may be requested in any order. It is up to the judge's discretion as to whether riders will be asked to work the opposite way on the rail or whether the judge finds he is able to determine class placing without the additional rail work in the oppositie direction.

When riders are asked to come into the center of the ring and line up for pinning, the backup will not be required, if it has already been required in the individual pattern work.

So, there you have it, the basic requirements and procedures for each of the classes you may be aiming for. Now it's time to turn your attention to show ring attire for you and your horse, so turn to chapter ten.

DRESSING THE TEAM IN THEIR BEST:
Show Ring Turnout for Horse and Rider

After spending from one to two or even three months of slow, careful work preparing yourself and your horse as a performance team, it's time to start thinking about that show ring appearance, your "turnout." How can you be sure that both you and your horse will look your best to catch the judge's eye? The best performance in the world will lose points if you present a sloppy or dirty appearance. Neat, clean, coordinated, polished — these are the words that should describe you on show day.

WHAT SHOULD THE RIDER DO TO PREPARE HIS MOUNT THE DAY BEFORE THE SHOW?

Just as you would bathe and get your hair cut or styled before dressing for a big date or event, so your horse deserves the same type of attention before making his big debut with you in the show ring. Visit your local tack store or check horse equipment catalogs and decide on the right type of horse shampoo for you. There are many brands on the market. It is important that you use products designed for horses, so that you do not damage your horse's skin and coat by applying a harsh and possibly harmful product. Your horse's skin is very sensitive, and he needs the essential oils in his coat to make him shine. Therefore, you should be careful to follow the directions on whatever bottle of equine shampoo you buy and be sure **not** to use water that is too hot. Not only would this temperature be uncomfortable for your horse, but it would also wash away too much of the natural oil in his coat. Warm water is okay. Very cold water would be hard for anyone to take. Have you ever gotten hit suddenly with a very cold shower? Yipes! Of course, be sure to rinse thoroughly.

Be sure, also, that your horse is used to getting a bath in the barn's wash stall area. Don't wait until the day before a show to have a royal battle with a horse who is petrified of even going into the wash stall, let alone getting squirted with a hose or sponged down with water. Find out ahead of time what your horse is used to and get him accustomed to what he will need to put up with to get ready for a show, long before the clock starts ticking a countdown of hours in your panic-stricken ears. If he needs to learn to allow you to squirt him down with a hose, start from his front legs and work at it gradually, holding him on a lead line, until he will let you squirt his whole body. Do not use too harsh a spray, and never squirt water in his ears or eyes. It is better to sponge his face or use a soft cloth and to work stroking downward, so as not to get soap in his eyes. It is also wise to work on his face while someone holds him on a lead line. Then, if he pulls back, he won't panic, because the handler can move backwards with him. This method will save a lot of battles and resentment on the part of the horse. Think how you would feel if someone squirted you in the face, when you didn't understand what was going on or forced you to endure soap in your eyes. And what about you mare's udder or your gelding's sheath area? Don't expect your horse to stand for a harsh squirting down there, although some may without kicking out at you. Find out what he or she will tolerate. If you are uncertain about how to clean your horse's udder or sheath properly, consult your veterinarian. That's much better than getting kicked in the face as thanks for your clumsy efforts.

Your horse's mane and tail will also need conditioner to look their best. Again, consult your tack store or catalog and decide on the products you will buy well ahead of time and learn how to use them. Wash and rinse the mane and tale thoroughly before applying conditioner. Hooves may be polished with "hoof black" type polish or with clear polish. "Show Sheen" hair polish may be applied to the horse's body, but remember one thing. Show Sheen makes hair slippery, so don't spray it on the horse's body where his saddle pad and girth will rest, unless you want to be in for a slippery ride.

Clipping is another problem that must be attended to with calm, careful planning, to be sure that the job is done both correctly and safely. Visit your tack store or order one of the many good books on clipping from a catalog or consult with an experienced horseman who knows how to clip a horse for the particular classes in which you wish to show. Generally speaking, don't try this alone if you have never done it before. If the horse has never been clipped before, don't crosstie him and suddenly walk up to him with a set of noisy clippers in your hand, unless you want broken crossties and a panicked horse. Besides, you could get hurt, if your horse thinks those clippers are out to get him. It may take a few days to several weeks to get your horse used to clippers, if he has never been clipped.

One easy method to get him used to the sound is to allow a pair of clippers to run outside his stall, where he can hear the new, strange sound, but from where he can observe it in safety. Next, with a quiet helper holding him on a lead line in his stall, show him the clippers turned off, so he can sniff them. Then, quietly turn them on and **let the horse bring his nose to the clippers out of curiosity**. If you go after him with them before he trusts that they are not a threat, he may never want to get used to them, because he has not been given that chance to make the decision that they are no big deal. Once he is used to the idea, you can gradually lay your hand, holding the clippers, against his neck with the clippers off and then with them on, so he can feel the vibration. Slowly and gently, work your way from his neck toward his muzzle and then also from the neck to his ears. Watch out for sudden reactions, getting tangled in the cord, and making scary noises by bumping clippers against metal halter fittings.

Here are some general guidelines for clipping your horse for English and Western events. For both types of classes, the muzzle is clipped free of those long whiskers for a cleaner appearance. For English events, the mane is clipped away just behind the ears, at the pole, only about an inch or two to create a bridle path, a flat area on which the headstall of the bridle may lie smoothly. For Western classes, the bridle path can be clipped from the pole down the mane as far as four to six inches, allowing the horse a longer bridle path but also a cleaner profile and a chance to show his strong jaw line. This is especially true for Quarter horse classes, where the deep jaw is one of the breed's characteristic features.

The mane itself is pulled to about four inches in length. Do not cut the mane with scissors or you will have a blunt cut with ends that stick out every which way. Very unsightly. Ask someone knowledgeable to show you how to pull your horse's mane with a pulling comb to the desired length. Do not attempt to pull the entire mane in one day. Not only will you have sore fingers but your horse will have a sore neck. Do this gradually over a few days' time. The English horse's mane is worn on the right side of his neck. The Western horse's mane is worn on the left side of his neck, a practice passed down from the cowboy, who needed to rope cattle from the right side of the horse and who therefore didn't want to have the horse's mane getting caught in his rope.

Western riders do not braid their horse's manes, but English riders may do so if they choose, so, if you are showing English, you will want to learn how to braid properly to give your horse an added touch of polish. Again, there are a number of books available on this topic on the market. Book or no book, however, it is wise to have someone who has done this job a number of times help you out on your first try. Some horses take easier to standing still for this tedious procedure, while others need to learn to adjust to this beauty treatment gradually. You don't need to be the "fumble fingers of the year" trying to teach yourself to braid the day before the show or worse yet the morning of the show handling a horse who won't stand for this strange grooming ritual. Get help early and practice well ahead of time. You will save yourself and your horse a lot of fuss, not to mention a possible accident caused by your nervous carelessness and an irritated horse.

Next, turn your attention to the excess hair hanging behind the horse's fetlock joint. This needs to be clipped away to show a clean, elegant leg. Be careful to have someone show you how to do this without getting "steps" in the layers of hair as you trim. Usually, if you turn the clippers to stroke gently down with the direction of the hair growth and don't take off too much at once, you can accomplish this without having the finished product look choppy. Also, you can carefully trim the hairs hanging down onto the hoof from the coronary band, to give a crisp, neat appearance to the hoof itself.

Tails may be shown free and full in both English and Western events, or the first few inches on either side of the dock of the tail may be braided together to form a little braid in the center of the tail a few inches long. This practice makes the tail look slimmer and less bushy and shows off the hind quarters more elegantly. It's a nice touch, but it is optional. The bottom end of the tail is never cut with scissors (unless you are showing dressage, which is a whole different story in itself). If the horse's tail is ragged on the bottom, pull the ragged edges to even it up. During your regular daily grooming, be careful not to break hairs by yanking a comb through the hair. Gently brush the tail, working from the bottom up, or separate the hairs with your fingers. It takes a long time to grow a long, healthy, beautiful tail, so don't abuse it with harsh grooming. Keep the tail conditioned to protect it. Some people even purchase a tail bag (sold at tack stores and in catalogs) for the horse to wear on the end of his tail while he is in his stall, to prevent the horse from breaking hairs as he swishes his tail at flies. One easy way to help your horse's mane and tail and his whole coat look their best is to condition them from the inside out. Add an ounce or two of corn oil to his grain every day. In a few weeks watch and see how his coat starts to develop a nicer shine. That oil, of course, can't replace good grooming, but it can help enhance the picture.

The next big questions, of course, concern your horse's tack and your show ring attire and the picture they create together in the judge's eye.

WHAT KIND OF TACK AND WHAT KIND OF ATTIRE WILL YOU NEED FOR EACH SHOW RING CLASS, WESTERN OR ENGLISH?

Whether you have just closed the deal on a brand new mount for this show season or whether you are determined to give old Sonny just one more try, you need to devise a plan that will present your package to the judge in the most favorable light.

We have all seen time and time again a cleverly packaged product, that is both eye-catching and neatly wrapped, outsell a competitor's more cost-efficient product because of colorful and attractive packaging. You, as a competitor in the show arena marketplace, must attempt to catch the judge's eye and create a favorable impression in those few precious minutes that you have as a competitor in the show ring. To do this you must focus on the areas of Attire, Tack, Fitness, and Form, attempting to enhance your team's positives and downplay your negatives to present the best possible package when you enter that show arena and move before the judge!

Choosing colors, shapes, and sizes of show clothing that enhance your show mount's color, size, and movement should be your first priority. For example, blues, greens, beiges, and rusts are great color combos for a sorrel or chestnut colored animal, while red, black, teal, and pinks are good color choices for a gray or black horse. Bay and brown colored horses tend to match up with a wider selection of colors and can usually be shown in most of the colors mentioned above.

Once you choose a color family to work from, select shapes, sizes, and patterns that enhance both you and your horse. For instance, if your horse is a short, choppy mover, picking bright colors with loud patterns in a Western class would only draw more attention to his cadence. If you have a shorter, squarer build, it might be wise to create a more solid-colored outift to help lengthen and slenderize your build. You may especially want to focus on detail when choosing an Equitation or Horsemanship outfit, where your form is being judged more than the appearance or movement of your horse.

Also, be sure that your show clothing fits well and is the correct length. Too tight clothing only draws attention to a weight problem, and sloppy fitting attire takes away from a neat impression, whether English or Western. Too loosely fitting clothes also may create the illusion that your horse is rough or speedy since they tend to move as he travels and flap more than properly fitted garments.

To save in the expense department, try shopping the bargain stores or sales once you have decided on a color scheme and pattern. Also check show newsletters for used clothing for sale or ask people in your local club where you can pick up used attire that is in good condition. Tack shops also sometimes sell used items on consignment. Many riders may outgrow or tire of an item after one show season offering a perfectly good piece at a greatly reduced price.

Remember, color, fit, your size and build, and your horse's build and movement, along with your piggybank will all play an important part in what attire and accessories you will choose for entering the show arena. If you are unsure how to coordinate an attractive show outfit, try consulting your trainer, lesson instructor, local tack shop, or 4-H leader. These industry leaders may be able to help or at least steer you towards someone with the expertise to make your appearance a blue-ribbon winner!

Basic Western Pleasure attire requirements for Open and Quarter Horse shows are long-sleeved shirt and pants with Western boots, cowboy hat, and tie. Chaps are optional, but they are required to look the part, since almost everyone wears them in all Western events. Detail equipment such as gloves or spurs are always at the option of the rider.

Basic Hunt Seat attire for Open and Quarter Horse shows is a light-colored (white or pastel) ratcatcher shirt with breeches (acceptable colors being buff, rust, dove gray) or jodphurs with high English boots or jodphur shoes. Black, navy blue, or brown hunting cap is mandatory with a traditional style hunt coat in a conservative color. A tie or choker is required. Again, spurs and bats are optional, but spurs must be of the unrowelled kind. Check individual rule books on both Western and hunt seat attire for any deviation from the basic requirements. Some breeds may specify attire criteria known only to that breed or club.

Tack specifications, on the other hand, can vary greatly from breed to breed and area of discipline. For instance, in a Western Pleasure class, one breed may allow a 4 1/2-inch port in a bit with 9 1/2-inch shanks, while another breed may only allow a 3 1/2-inch port and 81/2-inch shanks. One style of hunt seat riding may allow a figure eight or a flash cavesson, while the other does not. Tack allowments certainly may differ greatly. Be sure to educate yourself on the proper equipment needed for your area of competition or ask your trainer to help you to learn the "ropes" when it comes to tack. Also, check to see what organization or association is sponsoring a specific show, so you will know by whose rules you must abide in order to compete succesfully. Western horses may be shown in a variety of Western bits, depending on breed or association rules. Hunt seat bits may be snaffle, kimberwicke, or pelham. The Western saddle should have a seat and skirts suited to Western Pleasure riding. Hunt seat saddles should be all-purpose rather than the close-contact jumping saddle, to allow the rider to attain the balance seat position on the flat and the jumping position over fences. Western reins for Pleasure classes are normally the six-foot length type. Avoid barrel-racing type reins, and check with your breed association on limitations for bosals and hackamores. Check also to see if there are any limitations or restrictions on type of English reins. Generally, you would want to avoid the rubber reins used for jumping in an English Pleasure or Hunter Under Saddle class, mainly for esthetic reasons. Saddle pads for the Western saddle may be color-coordinated with your attire and your horse's coat color. English saddle pads, however, should be standard white. More on saddle pads and saddles as we progress here.

First and foremost in the tack department is purchasing a saddle, bridle, and saddle pad that is well-fitted to your mount. Nothing is more bothersome to your horse than a saddle that pinches or rubs, because your horse will give the judge the impression that your horse may be sour or lazy, when he is actually uncomfortable. Choose equipment that is sturdy and fits.

Also, choose a color and size of saddle that enhances you and your horse as a team. Whether you are riding hunt seat or Western, choose a color and style that is in line with your breed and riding discipline. For instance, you don't want to choose a dressage saddle if you are riding Quarter Horse hunt seat. As stated above, an all-purpose English saddle works best for the classes you will be involved in. Nothing detracts more from your appearance than not looking the part. Select a saddle seat size that is comparable to your own size and weight and a saddle tree size that fits your horse comfortably, as explained in earlier chapters. Have your tack store owner assist you or take along an experienced helper if you are unsure. If you have a darker horse, and you are a Western Pleasure rider, some of the lighter oil saddles enhance a darker colored horse beautifully. However, if your budget only allows you one saddle until you are off to college, you might go with a less trendy medium brown tone since tack, like any other product line, tends to change in style and color popularity over time, thus affecting its resale value and its suitability for show ring competition.

Always choose a headstall that flatters and frames your horse's head. If your horse has a long head, for Western choose a headstall with a large browband that dips or has a futurity knot. This feature will help to break up the appearance of a too-long face. Try a headstall with more silver features in Western for a horse with a gorgeous head, while down-playing the "chrome" for a plainer-faced animal. In hunt seat, you can go with a more costly raised or braided headstall for the more flattering face and a flatter leather for the plainer horse.

When purchasing a saddle pad, try to use colors that will not only be generic enough to match a few of your new show outfits, but will still continue to coordinate well with the color of your horse. Again, in Western pads, choose patterns and shapes that will move well with the horse's cadence. Never go with a Western blanket or pad, for example, that works against the horse's natural movement, no matter how pretty it matches your outfit. If you would rather buy one "good" blanket or pad, you can go the route of simply matching the blanket or pad to the tack and horse and foregoing matching it with the outfit altogether. Hunt seat, with its plain, white pad, of course, is a much simpler problem.

Last, but certainly not least, is the importance of entering the show ring class with nothing but spotlessly clean tack. Even old or plain tack can be greatly revived with a little saddle soap,oil, and good, old-fashioned elbow grease. A clean and neat appearance, even with less than trendy clothes and tack, gives a rider way more mileage than brand new attire and tack that is dull, dirty, or is loose, ill-fitting, or sloppy. If you are uncertain about proper procedure for cleaning and oiling tack or for laundering horse clothing (pads, blankets, sheets, etc.) or dry cleaning show attire, talk to the tack shop owner who can advise you on the best products and procedures. Remember, neatsfoot oil can rot stitching and does darken leather, so be careful before you dump it on a light-oiled saddle that you want to keep light- colored. Also, remember that it is better to launder a saddle pad than dry clean it, because the chemical residue from the dry cleaning process can be very irritating to the horse's sensitive skin. In choosing clothing for yourself, if you are on a limited budget, remember that the cost of a garment increases each time it must be dry cleaned, while a machine washable piece of clothing is much less expensive to keep looking nice, provided you don't shrink it in laundering.

Fitness and fashion go hand in hand. It is hard to look great in a new outfit when both you and your horse are not "fitted up" properly. Fitting your horse up means having him in the correct work program with daily exercise and good nutrition, which has been emphasized throughout this book. Horses are like people. They are all individuals and respond differently to different situations, as you have learned. Be sure you are using a training program that is correct for your horse, along with the correct equipment, and you are far along on your way to success. If you really need help, seek out a reputable trainer, as has been advised in this book. An exceptional animal in the wrong program will rarely work up to his peak performance level, and a mediocre animal in a compatible work and nutritional program has been known to beat the more talented animal not working up to par.

Your level of physical fitness and your nutritional needs should also be a daily concern of yours, as you have also learned in earlier chapters. Being physically fit and strong also helps you to develop more as a rider, and keeping your weight within a normal range lets your horse move more freely while allowing you to profile a nicer picture to the judge. Eating properly allows you to acquire the nutrition and energy you need for strength and stamina and overall good health so that you may continue in a sport that requires drive, discipline, and endurance, not to mention quick thinking, things that are hard to attain without exercise and a healthy diet.

Remember too, that once you are in that saddle and in that show ring, a balanced seat and correct posture not only look pretty but also help to smooth mistakes made by the horse and

give the rider a poised and confident appearance. A polished rider can "make up" for a lessor mount and bring out the best in a
talented one. Once attire, tack, and fitness have been attended
to, proper form in the arena certainly puts the "icing on the cake"
for you and your mount as a performance team. Many times, just
a few simple changes in your posture can tremendously improve
the impression you make on a judge. Some riders are not aware
of habitaul hand and face gestures or slumping shoulders, for
example, that detract from their appearance. Sometimes having
a good ground person to point out a negative is all that is needed
to correct it. Just as you use your skills to accentuate your horse's
positives and overcome his negatives, a mount that helps you
minimize your shortcomings is a plus as well.

While you are packaging your product, that is you and your
horse, for the show ring market place, try to keep a few common
sense guidelines in mind. As a whole, clothes, tack, training gimmicks, new styles in riding all tend to come and go with time. Try
not to package your product resulting in a "short shelf life." This
type of shortsightedness can be quite costly. Attempt to purchase
tack and clothing that reach beyond one show season. Select a
trainer with a good track record and sensible methods, if you do
work with a trainer. Trendy training tactics and riding styles tend
to go out as fast as they came in, leaving you to start all over again
with the next trend, still unable to get the best performance out
of your horse. It is more reasonable to stick to the basics of good
horsemanship and wise planning. Once you build your foundation, you can always add a new twist, if needed, one that is easily
changed when that trend dies out. It may be as small as an "in"
accessory, allowing you to take on the "new look" until a newer
fad takes its place.

Last, once you have finished your makeover of both horse
and rider, it is time to take your creation on a test run. Your first
horse show, perhaps a local schooling show, should be a good in-
dicator of what changes you will keep and what finishing touches you may want to add or subtract from your show ring
appearance. As with anything else, there will be a period of trial
and error, of additions or deletions. But, by focusing on and
working to perfect your attire, tack, fitness, and form you will be
much closer to delivering that impression which will send you
and your horse home from a show wearing that blue ribbon.
Now, you are ready to concentrate on chapter 11, your strategies
for the day of the show itself.

THE SHOW RING AT LAST:
Startegies and Expectations on the Day of the Show

Throughout this book, the authors have shown you how to lay a solid foundation for yourself and your horse through daily training and pre-show preparation. Now it is time to focus on the day of the show itself, from trailering and settling in at the show grounds to warm-up time and, finally, to actual strategies for performance in particular classes.

WHAT DOES THE RIDER DO TO PREPARE HIMSELF OR HERSELF AND THE HORSE TO PERFORM AT THEIR BEST, IN THEIR TRAVEL TO THE SHOW GROUNDS AND ONCE THEY ARRIVE AT THE SHOW GROUNDS?

First, make sure you have competent help in trailering the horse and that your horse is used to trailering in the type of trailer that you will be using. Plans for both of these things must be made sometimes weeks in advance.

Here are some suggestions for preparing your horse for trailering. You may need to have someone knowledgeable set up a trailer for you and your horse at your barn and then show you how to practice loading and unloading the horse. Never practice loading a horse on a trailer that is not hitched to a vehicle. It won't be stable and safe enough. You want to avoid accidents, not cause them. Also, avoid people who want you to beat and yell at your horse to get him to load. Such actions only make the horse associate the trailer with punishment. Why would he even want to go near a place where he thinks he will be punished for no reason he can figure out?

Some horses perceive a trailer as a dark hole. Some won't haul on a narrow, two-horse trailer but will do fine with the center partition removed. Some horses do best when traveling in a big stock trailer, especially young horses or those trailering for the first time. Some do better finding their balance if they are left loose in a stock trailer rather than traveling with their heads tied up front at the hay rack. Of course, if the trailer is a two-horse, allowing the horse to move freely may just invite him to get himself in trouble if he turns himself around and gets wedged in sideways during the trip. You don't want him to panic, start fighting, and hurt himself or even turn the trailer over! Find out what experiences your horse has had in the past and go from there. If he has had a bad experience, you will have to teach him to trust a trailer because he trusts you. You may need professional help, especially if he has had a truly frightening experience in the past.

If your horse is unfamiliar with trailering or has had a previous bad experience, he must be introduced gradually. Perhaps you can lead him up to it in a non-threatening way and feed him some hay near it. Then, he may eventually munch some hay on the trailer's ramp, if it is not a "step-up," and, finally, he may be content to munch some goodies while standing in the trailer itself. All of this could take days or weeks of patient work, spending about fifteen or twenty minutes a day. Don't rush him. Let him figure out that the trailer won't hurt him. When you think he is ready to load, you and a helper can coax him gently with a light touch of a whip on his back legs below the hocks, if he is not overly afraid of whips. Watch out! Don't overdo it and get kicked.

Also, it's a good idea to have an experienced person evaluate your horse's behavior around a trailer before you even start to practice with him, to determine if he is really fearful of a new situation or one that had previously given him a bad time. Maybe he is just an old hand at trailering who is bluffing you, because he just doesn't want to load. A horse who is just being stubborn may need a firmer hand from a more experienced person, but, again, don't put your trust in someone who wants to beat your horse unnecessarily. Neither should you trust someone who thinks that you can pull a horse into a trailer. He will only panic and pull his handler off his feet. Very dangerous! Also, be sure you yourself know how to load and unload correctly and that you don't do something foolish like letting the ramp down and releasing the butt bar or butt chain if the horse's head is still tied. He may try to back up, snap the trailer tie, and panicking, fly backwards out of the trailer, to land on his back or haunches. Ouch!

Once he will load and unload calmly, you may have someone haul him on a few short rides in the neighborhood, just to get him accustomed to keeping his balance when the vehicle is in motion. When he comes home and unloads calmly from these little trips successfully, be sure to praise him and even treat him to some munchies.

Now, let's take a look at the person who will be trailering your horse. If a responsible professional is trailering your horse to the show, you probably do not need to worry about the condition of his trailer and truck and whether he knows how to haul horses safely. His trailer's floor will be solid and safe, its latches and partitions will be in good condition, his equipment will have been inspected for road worthiness, he will have the proper insurance, and he will know how to load and unload horses without upsetting them unnecessarily. Of course, you should ask all of these questions when you first engage the professional's services, to determine if he is the man you want to trust. Then, you should not feel that you have to double check him on the day your horse is to be hauled, or he is not the professional you thought he was. You must, in addition, work out the cost to you (perhaps so much per mile, as suggested in the guide sheets in Chapter one) and find out if you will have access to the trailer as a base of operations for the entire show day. If the hauler is only going to drop you off and pick you up later, you had better find a helper with a station wagon or a large car or van or truck, who can provide you with a place to put your clothing and horse equipment for the day. Naturally, you also need to accommodate your horse, so you may need to rent a stall at the show ring facilities ahead of time. If there are none available, you may have to scrounge around to find a place to tie, rest, and feed your horse between classes. Planning ahead always makes for less tension.

If you are doing your own hauling, you must have sufficient, knowledgeable help for everything from driving to grooming, to watching the horse when you go to the refreshment stand to grab a snack. Whatever you do, **don't** take along someone as your main helper who is new to horses, just because he or she "just loves to be around horses and wants to learn." This is a mistake. You don't need to babysit an inexperienced person. You need to focus on yourself, your horse, and your performance. You need helpers you can count on in a pinch. If a novice wants to come along as an extra and knows how to stay out of the way and cooperate, fine. You must be firm on this. You will save a lot of time and trouble, frazzled nerves (your own and your horse's), and perhaps avoid some dangerous accidents in strange surroundings.

Before you haul, also make sure that you have the right safety equipment for your horse: leg wraps, head bumper, tail wrap*, and safety-release trailer tie. Make sure that your horse will tolerate leg wraps, head bumper, and tail wrap ahead of time by introducing him to these things gradually, with the help of another knowledgeable horseman. Make sure that you know how to use a safety-release tie and buy a good one that will work right in an emergency.

Last, before you head off to the show, try to obtain a show bill well ahead of the day of the show, if at all possible. This wise move will allow you to choose your classes ahead of time and estimate the time of day when you may be showing in a particular class, although horse show classes will vary with the size of the class and the amount of time the judge takes to make his or her decisions. Regardless of variation, any planning ahead you can do will allow you to plan your warm-up time and even your arrival time, if you are not planning to stable your horse at the show grounds the night before the show. Any preplanning you do will always help a lot to eliminate the show ring jitters that many competitors find so distracting on the day of the show.

If horse and rider can arrive at the show grounds the day before the show, your equine friend can have a bit more time to settle in and become comfortable in his temporary stall and new environment. He can adjust to strange bedding and the taste of different water. In fact, some competitors bring their own water from home. Why? Some horses just won't drink strange tasting water at first. The last thing you will need is a horse who must compete but who becomes sick from not having drunk sufficient water. Maybe your horse will do fine and accept new things readily, maybe not. Find out what you can about his habits and preferences before you get into a fix in a strange place. Get to know him. How picky is he? What upsets him? What tends to scare him? Remember the old saying: forewarned is forearmed. Besides, eventually, as you grow in experience and begin to attend shows of more stature or ones with money riding on the outcome, arriving the day before the show is one other variable you can control to help your horse to relax and perform better for you during the competition.

If you cannot arrive until the morning of the show, get there as early as possible, so that you and your mount are not rushed in preparing for your upcoming classes. At least your horse will have a little lead time to adapt to his new surroundings, instead of having to rush right from trailer to show ring.

As soon as your horse is unloaded and settled into his stall or comfortably tied to the trailer, secure a show bill or agenda of the day's events, if you have not been able to do so in advance of show day. Before you do this, remember, NEVER leave your horse without someone to watch over him and your valuable equipment. Any public place draws its share of thieves, but, what's even more important, in case your horse should get spooked at something or get himself into some kind of trouble, somebody knowledgeable has to be there to babysit. Once you have the show bill, you can decide which classes you will participate in and plan how much time you need to prepare for them. If you have never shown at this facility or under this judge or with this show management, get a feel from other exhibitors concerning how quickly the classes may move. This knowledge will help you gauge your prep time. You may also inquire at the entry booth about estimated start time for each class and how quickly the classes are expected to move. If, for example, you need two hours preparation and work down time before your Western Pleasure class, which will begin in only one hour, you may not have a chance to perform at your best and may not have a good enough ride to place in the ribbons. Of course, always place the importance of gaining experience and doing your best BEFORE the desire for a ribbon. Remember, if you work intelligently, you and your horse will eventually be in the ribbons. You want to be able to say to yourself: if it's worth doing for the ribbons, it's worth doing right.

Okay. Now comes the next big question:

HOW DO YOU PREPARE YOURSELF AND YOUR HORSE TO ENTER THE SHOW RING?

First, let's take a look at you. Are you a nervous wreck? Are you too excited to think about where you packed what piece of equipment? Way before the day of the show, you should sit down with the people who will help you and plan who will help you do what. Included in this strategy should be who will help keep you focused if you tend to be nervous or excited and who will keep you on schedule if you tend to take forever to do things and who will help you organize if that's not your strongest talent. Just as you observe your horse's behavior patterns, you should observe your own. Then, plan ahead. Also, decide firmly within your group to remain positive and upbeat and not to turn into whiners or negative thinkers. Little problems can become funny stories later instead of disasters, if you keep a positive attitude. Then, when you get to the show, stay away from people who may destroy this positive attitude. Stay away from spectators or competitors in the warm-up or refreshment areas who will crush your confidence or distract your focus. If you must talk with them, ignore their attitude and stay pleasant. Keep thinking: mind over matter; if you don't mind, it doesn't matter. If you do these things, you will find that the butterflies in the pit of your stomach will either disappear or will be greatly reduced. Naturally, since your horse can sense your mood, he will perform better with a positive, focused rider. Last, make sure you take care of yourself. Get enough rest the night before the show. Eat properly and drink enough fluids, if it's a hot day. Relax yourself and your horse in the shade between classes whenever you can to take the pressure off. For the horse, that also means removing the saddle or at least loosening the girth while he stands and waits, so the pressure will be let off the blood vessels in his back. This procedure may help avoid a sore back later.

Once you have your head together, you can concentrate on warming up your horse. You may want to wait until closer to the time you will enter the show ring to actually dress in your show clothes, so that you do not have to worry about getting them dirty while you tack up and warm up your mount. Just don't wait until the last minute to change clothes. Then, you'll spoil all the effort you have put in by reducing it to a mad rush. Not very wise.

First, you will need the lunge line and your lunge whip. To help your horse get the kinks out of his muscles, you can lunge him away from the noise of the crowd and competition with just a halter and line for about ten minutes in each direction. This will allow him to play on the line and get his spooks out as well as loosen up his muscles. Then, you should tack him up and lunge him for about another ten minutes in each direction. Remember the training principles that were presented to you in earlier chapters and try to make him feel that the procedures for tacking up and warming up on the lunge line are just like home, nice and relaxed.

By now you should be well-acquainted with your horse's temperament and athletic ability. As you lunge, gauge your animal's energy level. If, after twenty minutes of lungeing, he is still cantering when you ask for trot, he needs more time on the line. You should work him until he is relaxed with his attention focused on your commands. If he tends to be "cold backed," * he will have a chance to relax his back muscles and accept the saddle on the lunge line, so that you don't have to fight him once you are in the saddle. If you have never taken your horse to a horse show, plan roughly to do about twice as much preparation as you would do at home to allow for the horse's increased nervousness. If all this careful observation sounds like a lot of trouble, remember, it is much easier to work with a horse who has had the edge worked off him so that he will pay attention than to try to manage a nervous, "high," thousand-pound basket case.

Next, consider what class you will be showing in first and how you need to have your horse move, as you finally begin to get his attention on the lunge line. If you are warming up for English Pleasure or Hunter Under Saddle, your horse's stride can be longer and more energetic with less collection than for a Western Pleasure class. Therefore, if the English class is first, don't work on his Western jog or slow lope on the lunge line. Concentrate, instead, on the English gaits. If in later classes, you will be showing Western, you can return to the lunge line to refresh his memory and refocus his attention on the other way of going. Basically, be sure that before you enter the ring, your horse is tuned for that particular event.

Last, don't try to teach your horse anything new at the show grounds. It's enough that he focuses on your cues. Give him that opportunity to warm up and come together for you and that time for you to tune into him as well. Naturally, you should also remember not to try to make him accept any new equipment on the day of the show either. Imagine how you would feel if you had to perform wearing something you weren't quite sure would feel comfortable or work quite right. Again, the key words are plan, plan, plan AHEAD.

Now, it's time to do some warm-up work under saddle. If the warm-up ring is too crowded or full of competitors who don't know or won't follow simple courtesy rules, find another place where you and your horse can concentrate. Follow the training principles you have learned in earlier chapters. Don't try any new techniques and don't upset your horse with anxious moves.

Once you have him and yourself completely ready, you can check the warm-up ring again to see if it looks safe and sane or as crazy as a circus (they are sometimes). If the warm-up area looks manageable, give your horse one last spin there in tuning him up for the show ring. Then, find a spot near the entry gate, out of the way of traffic, and get ready for your debut.

In the minutes left before the competitors are called to enter the class, go over your performance in your mind. Think positive thoughts. Also, arrange to have your helpers meet you at this point for some very important strategy conversation. By this time, you should be dressed in your show ring attire and your helpers should have pinned your show number on you and wiped off any telltale dust from you or your horse. A little extra spritz of fly spray might be needed or an adjustment to your chaps or an extra hat pin for your hat. Get everything just right. Then, talk quietly about your research. What? Yes, research. Research on: what the judge is like, what the ring footing is like, what distractions may be on the rail on the spectators' side, and what the other competitors look like. Here's what you need to watch for.

Does this judge like a particular kind of movement or conformation type in a horse or a particular kind of rider? Has the same rider and horse team been winning a lot of classes? Why? If you have not had the time, somebody on your crew should have been keeping their eyes open. Remember, you are not getting together for idle gossip or to criticize the judge or the competitor. You are just trying to fill in your knowledge and maybe help your own performance. Naturally, you can't change your horse's way of going in a minute or make him a different color if the judge seems to like bays and sorrels (chestnuts) while you are riding a paint, but try to look beyond the obvious. Watch for what winning competitors have been doing. Is it their smooth transitions, their confident air, their consistency? Has anyone overheard what this judge's preferences might be? People always talk. Listen and evaluate.

Ring surface should also be a consideration as well as distractions to avoid or be ready for on the spectators' side of the rail. If somebody is sitting in the bleachers with a big yappy dog, you will have to be sure to keep your horse's attention as you go by that spot. If there's a big mud puddle on the rail and your horse likes to jump puddles, you can bet he will in these strange surroundings. Can you maneuver gracefully around it or ask him to go through it without looking bad to the judge? Will the "white noise" (that low-pitched hum) coming from the sound system's speakers set your horse off? Can you walk around the outside of the show ring and show your horse the potential trouble spots ahead of time? Bogey men tend to disappear for you and your horse when they are calmly faced outright. Can you manage to get your horse into the show ring for a practice run during a lunch or snack break for the ring crew and judge or between classes when the ring crew is setting up jumps or other obstacles or taking them down?

Last, what about the other competitors? Whose horse is a bigger mover than yours? Who is riding a pony with the stride of an inchworm? If you are entering a Western Pleasure class, don't get stuck behind the slowest mover in the class, if your horse moves a little faster or has a longer stride. Don't get stuck behind a kicker or someone who will spoil your performance with a troublesome mount. In other words, PLAN which competitor you will be in front of and behind as best you can. Then, when your class is called to enter, try to be the second or third person who enters the ring and go in putting forth your very best. Chances are, the judge will take a look at each individual rider and horse as they enter the ring. You want to make a good impression as well as be in a physical position that is easily remembered. In other words, don't get lost in the crowd. That brings up the next question:

WHAT STRATEGIES SHOULD THE RIDER USE ONCE HE HAS ENTERED THE SHOW RING?

First, if you have to school your horse in the show ring because he is misbehaving or becoming a danger to others, accept the fact that you will not be in the ribbons. If you know that you will have to blow the class to correct your horse, then do it, but don't get angry or flustered about it. Make it a simple, necessary correction. Chalk the class up to experience for you and your horse and go on from there. It's not the end of the world. However, remember, you have entered the class to be judged, so try to do your best to give a show ring performance. Don't give up and start correcting your horse for every little imagined imperfection in his performance. Have confidence. Think positive. Trust yourself and your mount. Feel your horse move underneath you. Think about working as a team, as a unit. In rail work, try to stay on the rail and try not to let your horse race past other competitors. Go deep into your corners, rounding your horse around your inside leg. In individual work, keep your focus on what will be your next move. Don't start fretting about the fact that you are alone in that ring performing before a bunch of people. You are doing your best. Be proud of yourself and your mount.

When you are working on the rail, listen to the announcer's commands. Keep in mind that your horse has ears too though, so don't tense up and think you must jump to do what is asked instantly. Such action will only make your horse anticipate the next move, and he'll end up getting tense too. He will begin to realize that every time he hears that announcer a change is on the way. He may even get to making a change on his own, whether it's what you would have asked for or not. Therefore, as explained in chapter 9, wait until the horse in front of you has made the change in gait called for, then calmly ask you horse to make his transition. You should be following the horse in front of you at a distance of one to two horse lengths for safety sake. This positioning will allow you time and space to maneuver correctly. If you or your horse makes a mistake on the rail or in individual work, put the mistake behind you and concentrate on your next move. If you have disqualified yourself for first place, you may still earn a ribbon, provided your error did not indicate your being eliminated entirely from competition and being asked to leave the ring. Even if you do blow the class badly and are asked to leave the ring, keep your head up. Behave courteously and professionally and learn from your experience. Don't compound a bad run by being a bad sport. Remember, even the best horses and riders have bad runs. Maybe other riders made mistakes too. Think of how you can work to make things go better next time.

In the line-up in the center of the ring after rail work, try to keep your horse and yourself in a state of calm attention. When the judge approaches the horse next to you, give your horse a tiny touch on the bridle and perhaps a very light touch with both legs to let him know that he will be asked to make a move soon. Don't cause him to step out of "square" position. Just quietly alert him. Then, when the judge gets to you, your horse will be focused and ready to do the final backup smoothly and calmly. You may even be pleasantly surprised by the judge's decision at the moment when the ribbons are awarded. One of those ribbons may belong to you and your horse. "It ain't over 'till it's over." Even if you haven't won a ribbon though, behave like a polished competitor even as you leave the ring.

If yours is an older horse who has special problems and has become ring sour, as some older horses do who have had a long history of showing, you may want to take him to a few schooling shows first, where you will be able to iron out his rough spots. Refer to Chapter Nine again and rethink your performance after each class. You may even want to make notes on what kind of individual style the judge seems to favor to help you in preparing for your next show under his or her eye. If instead, you decide it's time to upgrade to a new mount after the show season is over or that the time has come when you must get out of horses for a while, it's time to turn to chapter 12 here.

DECIDING TO SELL:
Moving Up or Moving Out

What makes a rider decide to sell his or her horse? There comes a point when no matter how attached a rider is to his mount or how well they have done in the show ring as a performance team, they must part with one another. This happens sometimes for several different reasons. In many cases, the rider simply outgrows the mount physically. The rider becomes too tall or too large and simply does not "fit" the horse like he used to. In other cases, the rider outgrows the horse mentally, because the rider's talent enables him to move up and on with show competition, but the horse's talents have been exhausted and can take the rider no further in competitive circles. Perhaps the horse has suffered an injury which will limit his ability to compete, or perhaps he is just getting too old for further competition. In yet other situations, the rider has reached a point in the financial road beyond which he cannot travel. He must sell his horse because he can no longer afford him or because he faces the upcoming costs of a college education or some other urgent need. Neither he nor his family is able to provide the continued support for the horse in time or money. Perhaps he must turn his attentions away from the horse world entirely for a period of time in his life.

Friends may be telling him that he should never give up on his equine friend, while his parents and more experienced horsemen may be insisting that emotional attachments to the horse must be severed for the benefit of both horse and rider. You, the horse's owner, may be torn between your own needs or goals and the bond that has grown between you and your equine friend. You have been through a lot together, and he has probably taught you as much as you have taught him. You are also most likely worried about what will become of him, how you will find him a good home. Dealing with your own emotions is one thing. In a practical aspect, though, what should you, the rider, do?

163

Talk the decision over respectfully with everyone involved. Make a list of good points and bad points for each type of possible decision and a list of possible uses your current horse could be put to. Would he be a child's first horse, if he is older and slowing down? A breeding prospect, if you own a mare who has been injured and is no longer sound? A mount for a rider in a different discipline than the one you wish to pursue? A donation for a riding for the handicapped program in your area? Seek the advice of your veterinarian or another respected horse professional who can give you an objective opinion, unaffected by the bias of your family and friends and the confusion of your own thoughts. Then, sit down with your parents and come to the final decision, based on what is truly best for all involved, not on what you wish could be the best scenario. Then, move forward with the decision and take action, with the help of your parents and more experienced horsy friends, who have added years of wisdom and experience in the everyday world of dealing with other people who will become your prospective customers for your mount or prospective sellers of a mount you may be interested in buying. Sometimes the right thing to do is the hardest thing to do, but it is still the right thing. Inside of yourself you will find the wisdom to live with the decision you make, if it is truly the right one.

Whatever the reasoning for selling your current horse and buying another one, once you and your family have decided that this must be done, be sure that you map out a plan of future goals about how you will proceed from this major decision.

HOW DOES THE RIDER DEVELOP A PLAN FOR MARKETING HIS HORSE?

If you are upgrading to a new mount and need to sell your horse first to put those monies towards your new horse, then you should focus on marketing your horse before you shop for a new equine teammate. You may spend many hours looking only to find that the horse you have chosen for purchase has been sold before you were able to gather your monies together from the sale of your current mount. Concentrate on the animal you have at hand first and then move to the next step, a different horse. Whether you are moving out or moving up, define a realistic price for your horse before you begin to attempt to sell him. It may sound harsh and cold to begin thinking of your friend in terms of dollar signs, but you will have to get used to this idea sooner or later. You may be able to console yourself a little by insisting that you will only sell him to a good home (as well you should), but the truth is, seeing your horse, your friend, as a product to market is going to take some getting used to. Relying once again on friends and family, though, may help you make the mental and emotional adjustment. You will need to decide what you need to get if you are selling out, and if you are up-grading, set a figure that you will need to obtain to help you achieve your future goals in a better mount. Either way, the key word here is "realistic."

Many owners become what is termed "barn blind," when they are emotionally attached to their animals and tend to over-price the horse. He may be a trusted friend, but in the market-place, he is also a product with a price tag. Your love for him will not make him worth a phenomenal figure, so be realistic about his abilities. Also, if you have spent time and money on your own education, for example, you certainly would not expect to get that back on your very first job. In the same respect, be accurate about your horse's worth regarding the recovery of training fees, vet fees, boarding fees, and shoeing fees when you resell your animal. You can't expect to recover every dollar you have spent on him. To help you understand this business aspect of horse ownership, consider your horse as you would a car or house. If you have purchased a car at a fair price but have replaced parts and have given it a paint job, you would be able to ask an even higher fair market price for your improvements. You would not expect to be able to recover the cost of regular maintenance of the vehicle. Or what about a real estate investment? If you bought a house in fair condition but didn't keep up on the maintenance, would you expect to make money on that property at selling time? Would that investment bring you a higher price? Likewise, you must ask yourself if your horse is in top shape in order to be put on the market. Has he had additional training and acquired a better show record since he has been in your hands? Have you stopped showing and left him field boarded for months or even a year to save money while you decided what to do with him and while he got more and more out of shape? Besides, if you want to find him the good home he deserves after all he has given to you, shouldn't he be looking his best, with his best foot (or rather "hoof") forward? As a friend, does he deserve to be neglected just because you have now decided to sell him? Should you discard his care as if he were an old toy you are tired of?

You must be both fair and realistic about pricing your animal. The price could make the difference between selling your horse within a month or within a year. Consider his age, size, conformation, movement, disposition, attractiveness, breed, show record, training, and competitiveness. Measure these factors in light of what you have paid for the horse plus any improvements or any problems which have arisen. All of these considerations will help you determine a fair asking price for your mount.

If you decide to tackle this project solely on your own and without the help of an equine broker or trainer, you will need to venture into the realm of advertising. Establish an advertising budget of twenty per cent of your selling price. You may not need to spend quite this much on advertising, but again, being realistic will give you plenty of room in your budgeting. Usually, a more expensive model will eat up your budget way faster than a run-of-the-mill guy. Once you have defined your budget, examine the trade publications of your breed or multi-breed publications and decide where to promote your "Old Ned." These publications, as well as the advice of friends who are more experienced, can give you an idea of whether the price you have set is in line with what the market will bear.

If Ned is priced at $2000 or less, stick with putting a "for sale" classified in as many local papers as you can in the "horses for sale" or "livestock" section of the classified. With a less expensive mount, try the local free papers too. You can interview each prospective buyer yourself and even check him or her out through your own local contacts and the "horsy grapevine" to see if your horse would have that good home with this new person. You can also explain any special needs your horse may have. At $2000 to $6500, you can try putting classified ads in the back of your pertinent trade publications and hanging up printed flyers at shows, indicating the breed and show history of the animal. **(See the sample flyers at the end of this chapter for ideas.)** You can also network by phone and fax to local trainers and brokers, letting them know that you are willing to pay the standard ten per cent commission if they were to send you a buyer. Stress also, of course, the type of rider and owner you would like to see your horse with, to be more certain of finding him the kind of home he deserves. All of these methods are still keeping you in the lower end of your advertising budget, since the yield of your sale is not tremendous in itself. In addition, don't forget your good old word-of-mouth advertising along that "horsy grapevine." Tell everyone you talk to at shows or who is in the horse industry, such as your farrier and veterinarian. These equine professionals have access to many people in your target market during their day's work and may be able to connect you with a potential buyer for no charge at all.

At the $6500 to $12500 price range, you will begin to narrow your target market to more serious competitors and investors. It will take more money and effort on your part to close your sale. With a more expensive mount, you may want to seek the help of a professional horse broker who specializes in matching up buyer and seller and who is familiar with selling a horse in this price range. The broker will also be able to do an accurate appraisal or market analysis of the animal to determine its true net worth. If you still choose to market the animal on your own, be prepared to purchase a nice display ad with a photo in a larger trade publication. Also, begin to beef up your networking to outside of your immediate area, calling trainers who may have students who may be interested in a horse like yours. Naturally, this approach allows you to query the trainer or broker about the type of person as well as the type of rider a prospective buyer may be. If possible, continue to show your horse for further exposure and promotion, until he is sold. The more outside exposure you can give the horse through classified and display advertising, telemarketing, print advertising, and show promotion, the better your chances of getting the horse sold.

In the $12000 and up range, you would be wise to lean on an industry professional for additional support. If you don't want to take your horse to a trainer or consignment barn, if you don't want to be separated from him until you absolutely have to, at least list your horse with an equine broker or maybe several brokers throughout the country. This usually consists of a nominal listing fee and of supplying the broker with a good video and pictures with which to market the horse, since he will not be stabled in the broker's barn. The broker will also want to know all of the particulars on the horse such as show record, training, size, temperament, age, breed, movement, vices, health records, and any other information you can supply, since the broker will unable to view the horse personally, due to time and distance constraints. Of course, you can make your own video and then do a mass mailout to prospective trainers on your own.

If the horse stays with you entirely while you are marketing him, remember again that he will sell easier and faster if he is in top shape. Think back to the car without the paint job scenario. Even the best of pros have a hard time seeing through a thick hair coat and lack of muscle tone. Keep up your horse's work routine and be sure to blanket and hood him during the winter months to keep him looking slick, not only because you want to care for him properly. And when you do close that sale with a look to upgrading, be sure that you make a wise buy and take a step up, not a horizontal move, so that all of your time and effort really pay off.

Once you do sell your mount, you will want to have a legal bill of sale for the buyer and will want to ensure that you are paid the agreed price. **See the sample bill of sale in the appendix.** Now read on further to discover the answers to questions about searching for a new horse and about finalizing the sale of a horse.

HOW DOES THE RIDER SEARCH FOR A NEW HORSE?

The search for the perfect horse can be both a tedious and difficult task, even for the most accomplished horse person. Looking for a more specialized prospect, such as Western Pleasure or Hunter, can be even more taxing. Here are some basic guidelines. Begin your horse hunting by locating reputable individuals within the horse industry who deal in the type of horse for which you are searching. Look through trade publications, ask friends for referrals, and network on your own by talking to other horse owners and exhibitors, clubs, and organizations (the horsy grapevine again). Also, observe which trainer and his students are winning in the classes in which you wish to show. Not only do you want to deal with an honest and reputable person but also with someone who has the know-how and talent to offer you a competitive and safe mount.

When you have decided upon several individuals or farms with which you feel comfortable, set some buying guidelines for yourself, before you ever set foot in their barns. Would you consider a green horse? Do you have the time and talent to finish a green horse? Do you have the money for someone else to finish the horse for you, or would you need a finished product? Are you a bigger person who needs a sturdier animal or are you petite, requiring a more refined, streamlined horse? Do you have a color or breed preference? Do you have a particular bloodline that appeals to you? Will your mount be showing in more than one type of class and thus need to be more versatile as an athlete? What is the show record of each prospect? The health record? What price range are you in? Don't spin your wheels going to look at a horse whose price is way out of your grasp. Go back and reread the earlier chapters of this book and redefine your talents and the needs you have in a mount at this point. Before you travel to a farm to visit a prospective horse, screen your choices by finding out the answers to as many questions as possible on the phone. If the horse is at a great distance, see if you can obtain a video of the prospect from the seller. Videos are especially handy in allowing you to take your time to compare different horses in the privacy of your home.

As stated earlier in this book, there is little chance of finding the perfect horse. Decide what you can or cannot live with and make your choices from there. If the first group of horses doesn't meet your requirements sufficiently, keep looking until you find a mount who meets more of your needs.

Now for the final question:

WHAT ARE THE DETAILS FOR FINALIZING THE SALE OF A HORSE?

Following a few simple rules of thumb will turn your sale or purchase experience into a pleasant memory instead of an unforgettable disaster. Once you have chosen a mount to buy or have decided on a buyer for your horse, clearly define the terms of the sale, whether you are dealing with a trainer, broker, or a private owner. Get every aspect of the agreement in writing, such as : the price of the animal, a contingency of a pre-purchase vet exam, any trial period arrangements, and terms of payment (deposit to hold, payment in full, financed by seller or bank, payment amounts, etc.). If you choose a more detailed situation, such as trying the animal on a trial basis or a payment plan, make sure you outline these terms in detail in the sales agreement. Consider such things as what happens if the horse you are buying dies or is injured while in your possession during the trial period or if your horse is injured or dies in someone else's hands or when each of your (or your horse's buyer's) monthly installments are due. If there are any disagreements between buyer and seller after the fact, both parties will have a document in writing to refer to. Also, a bill of sale or sales agreement can be used for tax purposes and should be included in your financial file.

Another good precaution to exercise when buying a horse is to use a check as your method of payment instead of cash or a cashier's check. Although paying with cash or the equivalent will release to you all of the horse's pertinent paperwork, such as registration papers, transfer report, and health records, paying with a check is a better short-term insurance plan. **(See sample registration papers in the appendix.)** If you are buying a horse and discover that he was misrepresented after you get him home, you can always stop payment on your check until your differences are resolved with the seller. If you pay cash when you purchase and pick up the horse, you will never be able to change what has already been solidified. Few sellers will rectify the situation once they have cash in hand. If you are selling the horse and your buyer pays by check, don't release the horse to him until you have called his bank to verify that funds are available in his account to cover the amount of the check he has written to you.

The last crucial factor of a horse purchase is to be sure that each step of the transaction occurs in a certain order. For instance, you would never pay for an animal before you have received the results of the pre-purchase exam. Therefore, to protect yourself against a price change, misrepresentation, or receiving a "defective" animal in both a mental and physical aspect, request to the seller that the transaction occur in the following manner. You should also consider the following guidelines if you are the seller marketing your own horse.

1.   Once you have agreed on a price, set up a day and time for the veterinarian (preferably your own) to administer the pre-purchase exam. Try to be present at the exam to get a firsthand account of possible problems or injuries. If you are a minor, have a parent or guardian present or an experienced horse person. If you can't be present, speak with the vet by phone to get a detailed account afterward.

2.   Once the pre-purchase results meet your satisfaction, arrange a day and time with the seller to pick up and pay for the horse. If you are the seller, arrange for your buyer to come and get the horse. Request that any terms of a verbal agreement be written into the bill of sale agreement. Check with your buyer's bank to verify the availability of his funds. If you are the buyer, when you arrive to take your new horse home, you should pay by check. Both seller and buyer should sign the sales agreement with both receiving a copy for their files. If you are a minor, you should have your parent or guardian on hand during the entire transaction, because a parent or guardian's signature will be required.

3.   Before the sale is completed, the buyer should request from the seller a background file of the horse, including such things as health records, farrier records, training program, clipping and hauling manners, and a list of possible vices. This should be presented in writing when the sale is completed.

4. If you or your parent or guardian requires an additional receipt for tax purposes, this should be obtained at the conclusion of the sale.

5. Names, phone numbers, and addresses should be provided of owner, trainer, and broker to all parties involved, in case any questions should arise.

If you follow the above procedures, you will have the reassurance of a safety net whether you are buying or selling a mount.

Last, if you have decided to continue to pursue your interest in horses with a new mount, be sure to use this book for future reference, and look forward to your next show season with a positive attitude and an organized plan for success. Happy riding!

GLOSSARY

AIDS: something used by the rider to communicate signals to the horse. The rider may use parts of his body, such as his hands, legs, weight distribution, seat, and back to cue the horse. He may also use his voice (although not in the show ring) and may employ a whip or spurs or even some training device like side reins to help in schooling his mount.

CANTER: one of the horse's gaits. A canter is the gait which has three distinct beats followed by a brief moment when all of the horse's feet are suspended, that is not touching the ground, before the next stride begins. The canter occurs on one lead or the other. That is, one side of the horse's body leads the other side. If a horse is on his right lead, the right side of the body is leading; if he is on his left lead, the left side of his body is leading. The right lead, for example, begins with the horse taking a step with his left hind foot. This is the first beat of the canter. The second beat occurs as the right hind foot and the left front foot move forward together. The third beat of the canter stride occurs as the right front foot steps forward by itself. Having the horse on a right lead for a right circle or turn allows him to use his right front leg to support his body on the turn. Thus, the rider finds that his ride is not only more comfortable but also safer, since the horse has no support and risks falling if he is cantering a right turn while on the left lead.

CAVALLETTI: specially designed training obstacles over which the horse may be asked to walk, trot, or canter in order to balance, extend, or collect his stride. Basically, a pole is attached at each of its ends to wooden X's, so that the height of the pole off the ground may be set at six inches, twelve inches, or even eighteen inches. Cavalletti may be set up on the ground in a particular pattern of three or four cavalletti in a row or even in a spiral pattern. The distance between the cavalletti should allow the horse to complete a stride at a given gait without having to scramble to keep going to avoid striking one of the poles with one of his hooves.

COLIC: abdominal pain which may be caused by a collection of gas in the bowel, a hard mass of food or feces in the bowel that has blocked the bowel, or a twist in the bowel that blocks the bowel. Colic is a serious illness and requires calling the veterinarian for assistance. Colic may be caused by stress or by the horse's drinking cold water or eating grain too soon after exercise. Symptoms the horse may show include pawing, biting at his sides, sweating around the shoulders and flanks, and a desire to roll.

COLLECTION: the act of asking the horse to round his spine and gather his stride into a shorter, more elevated shape. The beats of the stride, whether walk, trot, or canter, still stay the same, but the horse uses more of his energy to round and raise his body than to spread it out low to cover more ground.

CONFORMATION: the body type and particular physical features of the horse, which may referred to in terms of special features for his breed or in terms of weaknesses or strengths for performance in a particular equine sport.

COOL DOWN: the period during which the horse is walked either under saddle or in hand (on a lead line) to bring his respiration and heart rate back to normal after extended, strenuous exercise. The hotter the weather the longer the time needed.

CROUP: the rounded area at the top of the horse's hind quarters just behind his kidney area.

DIAGONAL: the pair of the horse's legs at the English trot to which the rider chooses to post to the trot, that is rise to the diagonal. Since the horse's legs move together diagonally at the trot, left hind / right fore and right hind / left fore, the rider rises to one diagonal or the other.

EXTENSION: the opposite of collection. The act of asking the horse to extend or stretch his stride to a long, low, ground-covering gait.

FLAT CLASS: a show ring class in which all performance work is done on the ground without any jumping involved.

FOUNDER: a sinking of the coffin bone inside the hoof, caused by inflammation and tearing of the laminae or supporting tissues inside the hoof. The condition is extremely painful to the horse and life threatening. The horse most often suffers the condition from eating too much grain, from allergy, from a portion of retained afterbirth in a mare, or from traveling over hard or rough surfaces during exercise. The horse will rock back on his hind quarters and refuse to walk forward on his front feet.

FROG: the triangular-shaped portion of the sole of the hoof, which expands and contracts as the horse steps.

GAIT: any of the horse's natural ways of moving: walk; trot / jog; canter / lope/; and gallop.

GASKIN: a muscle of the front of the upper portion of the hind leg. A well-muscled gaskin is one indication of a strong hind leg conformation.

GRADE: a term used to refer to a horse's breeding when he is not registered with any particular breed association and may be a mixture of two or more breeds.

HOCK: the joint of the hind leg half way up the leg, which is comparable to a human's ankle joint. Strong hocks are one indication of good hind leg conformation.

JOG: a slow, slightly collected trot used in Western riding.

LAMINITIS: an inflammation of the sensitive tissues in the interior of the hoof, which hold up the coffin bone. Laminitis often leads to founder, is very painful for the horse and is a serious illness requiring a veterinarian's care.

LATERAL: any sideways movement the rider may ask of the horse. The leg yield, the sidepass, the spiral, and all bending require lateral movement.

LEAD ON A CANTER: the side of the body with which the horse is leading. See CANTER above.

FLYING LEAD CHANGE: a movement in which the horse changes from one lead to another at the canter / lope without first breaking to the trot.

SIMPLE LEAD CHANGE: a movement in which the horse changes from one lead to another at the canter / lope after first breaking into a trot for a stride or two.

LOPE: a slow, slightly collected canter used in Western riding.

LUNGE: (also LONGE): exercising or schooling a horse by asking him to work in a circle around the handler at the end of a twenty- to thirty-foot line.

LUNGEING CAVESSON: a special kind of halter with rings on the noseband to which the handler may attach a lunge line to make it easier to lunge the horse properly.

NAVICULAR DISEASE: a disease of the small bone at the back of the hoof, which usually involves the degeneration of the bone and attached tendons, causing pain and chronic lameness in the horse.

ON THE BIT: an expression which refers to the horse's balancing his forward energy lightly on the bit as he strides forward in his movements and as he holds his spine in a particular shape.

PASTERN: the sloping bones of the leg just above the hoof, which angle backwards before meeting the next joint, the fetlock joint of the leg. Smooth, gently sloping pasterns are an indication of good conformation and and indication of a comfortably riding horse.

RINGBONE: a disease which involves changes in the coffin bone and the bones of the pastern. It causes lameness and may be caused by trauma or bad conformation in the horse.

RING SOUR: a term used to refer to an attitude in the horse which causes him to be unwilling to perform ring work. This is often caused by incorrect overdrilling of the horse in an arena.

RUNNING MARTINGALE: a training device which is a strip of leather which attaches to the center of the girth, and then splits into two strips of leather each with a ring on the end. The bridle reins are run through the rings and up to the rider's hands, so that the action of the rider's hands is transferred down to a lower action, near the horse's chest, thus helping to keep the head of a resisting horse lowered.

SIDE PASS: a lateral movement of the horse's legs in which he steps sideways while crossing the stepping leg over and in front of the standing leg.

SOUNDNESS: a term used to refer to a horse's physical health and his ability to perform in a given equine sport. A sound horse is a well horse but not necessarily a fit horse, for a horse can be sound but out of shape or condition, that is "soft".

SPLINT: a little lump or knob-like blemish on either side of the cannon bone on a horse's leg. It can result from a tearing of the tissue that holds the splint bone next to the cannon bone. When the tear is new, it is painful, and when the tear heals, a knob is created. It may or may not affect the action of the tendons near it, depending on how big the knob is. A splint injury is usually a "physical stress-related" injury.

STIFLE: the joint at the very top of the horse's hind leg before it joins his body. It is comparable to the human knee joint.

TACK: any piece of equipment used on the horse: bridle, saddle, and halter and lead are all pieces of tack.

TRANSITION: any change in gait from one gait to another. A horse should demonstrate smooth, fluid transitions, which are balanced and which are not rushed or awkward.

TROT: a two-beat gait in which the horse uses diagonal legs together: the left hind and the right fore, followed by a brief moment of suspension, followed by the right hind and the left fore, followed by a brief moment of suspension before the next stride begins.

TROTTING POLES: six-foot long poles laid on the ground, approximately four feet apart (depending on the individual horse's natural length of stride) and over which the horse is asked to trot as an exercise to balance, lengthen, or collect his stride. The poles may be set up in groups of three or four lying parallel with each other or in a spiral patter, if the horse is working on a circle.

WALK: one of the hose's gaits in which each foot is used in a separate step forward, so that the horse steps in an even four-beat rhythm, with only one foot in motion at a time and the other three feet on the ground. There is no brief moment of suspension at the the end of one stride before the beginning of the next stride. The horse moves right hind, left fore, left hind, and right fore as he walks.

BIBLIOGRAPHY

Blazer, Don. *Natural Western Riding*. Boston: Houghton Mifflin Company, 1979

Bradbury, Peggy and Steve Werk. *Horse Nutrition Handbook*. Houston: Cordovan Corporation, 1974.

Corley, G. F. *Riding and Schooling the Western Performance Horse*. New York: Arco Publishing, Incorporated, 1982.

Denby-Wrightson, Kathryn and Joan Fry. *The Beginning Dressage Book*. New York: Arco Publishing, 1981.

Frederiksen, A. K. *An Introduction to the Finer Points of Riding*. London: J. A. Allen and Company, Ltd., 1978.

Harris, Susan E. *Grooming to Win*. New York: Charles SCribner's Sons, 1977.

Klimpke, Reiner. *Cavalletti*. London: J. A. Allen and Company, Ltd., 1985.

MacDonald, Donald L. *Know the Anatomy of the Horse*. Omaha: Farnam Horse Library, 1971.

Museler, Wilhelm. *Riding Logic*. New York: Arco Publishing, 1981.

Straiton, E. C. *The Horse Owner's Vet Book*. San Francisco: Harper and Row, 1979.

Swift, Sally. *Centered Riding*. New York: St. Martin's Press, 1985.

Twelveponies, Mary. *Everyday Training: Backyard Dressage*. New York: A. S. Barnes and Company, Incorporated, 1980.

Watson, Valerie. *Trimming and Clipping*. London: Threshold Books, Ltd., 1986.

Williamson, Charles O. *Breaking and Training the Stock Horse*, 6th ed. Caldwell, Idaho: Caxton Printer, Ltd., 1968.

Young, John Richard. *The Schooling of the Horse*. Univer. of Oklahoma Press, 1982.

APPENDIX

All sample Fauna Forms were reproduced with the permission of Fauna Forms Inc. and can be ordered through Fauna Forms Inc. Cincinnati., OH 45236 (800) 543-4208.

Bill Of Sale Contract

This BILL OF SALE is to certify that on this_____day of_____19____, hereinafter referred to as Seller, has sold the animal_____, registration number_____. to_____, hereinafter referred to as Buyer , for consideration of the purchase price of $_____. Buyer & Seller mutually agree as follows:

1. The Seller guarantees that Ⓐ he has full power to sell the animal, Ⓑ the title is clear and free from liens and is unencumbered; and further, Ⓒ he will defend the same against the claim or claims of all persons who whomsoever.

2. Buyer agrees to purchase the animal as is. The Title shall be transferred at the signing of this BILL OF SALE and all responsibility of the animal shall transfer to the Buyer at that time.

3. This BILL OF SALE represents the entire agreement between the parties. No other agreements or promises, verbal or implied, are included unless specifically stated in this written agreement.

Additional guarantees or agreements should be individually initialled by Seller and Buyer, if none, check box l.

4. This BILL OF SALE is made in the State of_____, and shall be enforced and interpreted under the laws of this state. Should any clause above be in conflict with State Law, that individual clause shall be null and void.

When Buyer and Seller (and Buyers and Seller's parents or guardians, if Buyer and/or Seller is a minor) sign this Contract, it will then be binding on both parties.

DESCRIPTION OF ANIMAL			
SEX	YEAR BORN	BREED	COLOR, MARKINGS, BRANDS, TATOO'S, ETC.

Signature of Seller X _____ I.D._____ Date _____
                        Signature of Seller or Authorized Agent

If Seller is a minor X _____ Date _____
                        Signature of Parent or Guardian

Address _____

Signature of Buyer X _____ I.D._____ Date _____
                        Signature of Buyer or Authorized Agent

If Buyer is a minor X _____ Date _____
                        Signature of Parent or Guardian

Address _____

Witness X _____ Date _____

Witness X _____ Date _____

Deposit of $ _____ received on _____ by _____

Release From Liability Contract

This RELEASE FROM LIABILITY is made and entered into on this_____day of_____,
19___by and between_____, I hereinafter designated MAN-
AGER/INSTRUCTOR and _____, hereinafter designated RIDER; and, if
Rider is a minor, Rider's parent or guardian,_____. In return for the use to-
day, and on all future days, of property, facilities, and services of the Manager/Instructor, the Rider, his heirs, assigns
and legal representatives, hereby expressly agree to the following:

1. Rider is responsible for full and complete insurance coverage on his horse, personal property and himself.

2. Rider understands there are risks in and around equine activities, and, that an equine activity sponsor and/or equine professional and/or manager/instructor is not liable for an injury to, or the death of, a rider, and/ or a participant in equine activities resulting from the inherent risk of equine activities.

3. RIDER AGREES TO ASSUME ANY AND ALL RISKS INVOLVED IN OR ARISING FROM RIDER'S USE OF OR PRESENCE UPON MANAGER/ INSTRUCTOR'S PROPERTY AND FACILITIES including, without limitation but not limited to: the risks of death, bodily injury, property damage, falls, kicks, bites, collisions with vehicles, horses or stationary objects, fire or explosion, the unavailability of emergency medical care, and/ or the negligence and/or deliberate act of another person.

4. Rider agrees to hold Manager/Instructor and all successors, assigns, subsidiaries, franchisees, affiliates, officers, directors, employees and agents completely harmless and not liable and releases them from all liability whatsoever and AGREES NOT TO SUE them on account of or in connection with any claims, causes of action, injuries, damages, costs or expenses arising out of Rider's use of or presence upon Manager's/ Instructor's property and facilities, including without limitation, those based on death, bodily injury, property damage, including consequential damages, except if the damages are caused by the direct, willful and wanton gross negligence of the Manager/Instructor.

5. Rider agrees to waive the protection afforded by any statute or law in any jurisdiction (e.g. California Civil Code § 1542) whose purpose, substance and/or effect is to provide that a general release shall not extend to claims, material or otherwise, which the person giving the release does not know or suspect to exist at the time of executing the release.

6. Rider agrees to indemnify and defend Manager/Instructor against, and hold harmless from, any and all claims, causes of action, damages, judgements, costs or expenses, including attorneys' fees, which in any way arises from Rider's use of or presence upon the Manager's/Instructor's property and acuities.

7. Rider agrees to abide by all of Manager's/Instructor's rules and regulations, and rider is responsible for using protective gear; i.e. hard hat and boots.

8. If Rider is using Rider's horse, the horse shall be free from infection, contagious or transmissible diseases. Manager/Instructor reserves the right to refuse horse if not in proper health or is deemed dangerous or undesirable.

9. This Contract is non-assignable and non-transferable and is made and entered into the State of _____, and shall be enforced and interpreted under the laws of this state. Should any clause be in conflict with State Law, then that clause is null and void. When the Manager/Instructor and Rider (and Rider's parent or guardian, if Rider is a minor) sign this contract, it will then be binding on both parties, subject to the above terms and conditions.

I have read and understand this release.

X
_____
Rider's Signature

Manager's/Instructor's Signature

X
_____

Address & Telephone of Rider

Rider's Parent or Guardian (if Rider is a minor)
Description of Horse (if applicable)

_____

_____

_____

Training Contract

This **TRAINING CONTRACT** is made and entered into on this _____ day of _____ 19___ , _____ , by and between, _____ , hereinafter designated "Trainer," and _____ , hereinafter designated "Owner," and, if Owner is a minor, Owner's parent or guardian _____ . Trainer agrees to accept Owner's horse _____ Reg. No. _____ for training; and, it is the plan and intention of Owner to place this horse into training. For and in consideration of the mutual agreements hereinafter set forth, the Owner and the Trainer mutually agree as follows:

1. Owner shall pay Trainer for professional services as described below, the fee of $_____ per month or $_____ per day, for training and board, board alone being $_____ per month or $_____ per day, for a minimum of _____ months. A security deposit of $ _____ , payable upon execution of this Contract, shall be refunded within thirty (30) days after Contract is completed. Monthly rates and all other charges are subject to change upon thirty (30) days written notice to Owner.

2. Invoices are payable upon receipt. A late fee of $_____ will be charged if payment is received more than seven (7) days late; plus, a finance charge of 1½% per month (18% annually) will be charged on all accounts 30 days past due. If payment is overdue by ninety (90) days, Trainer is entitled to a lien against horse for amount due and shall enforce lien and sell horse for amount due, according to the appropriate laws of the state. On completion of this Contract, remainder of expenses are due and payable. Horse will not be released until all expenses are paid in full.

3. Trainer will use a veterinarian and farrier of his choice to provide ordinary and necessary care, unless Owner has requested his veterinarian_____ and his farrier _____ be used; however if they are unavailable, Trainer will engage his choice. All veterinarian, farrier and medicine expenses shall be paid by Owner.

4. Trainer shall train horse and perform all services in accordance with generally accepted professional standards. Trainer cannot and does not guarantee effect of the training program or that any particular results will be achieved, since this depends a great deal on the individual ability of each horse. Trainer shall furnish all labor, provide suitable facilities and care for horse in an ordinary manner with feed being determined by training schedule and individual's metabolism. Trainer has complete control over manner of training and shall take precautions for proper performance thereof.

5. Both parties agree that_____ (Farm), the Trainer, their agents and employees are not liable for death, sickness and/or accident including consequential damages to horse unless such death, sickness and/or accident was caused by the willful and wanton gross negligence of Trainer; and the Owner is not liable for death, sickness and/or accident including consequential damages caused by horse unless Owner had knowledge of horse's pre-existing problems which were the direct cause of such.

6. Horse shall be healthy and sound, free from infectious, contagion or transmissible diseases. A current negative Coggins Test, photostat copy of registration papers (both sides), veterinarian's health certificate, plus a health, worming and immunization record must accompany horse, if not, horse will be examined and/or tested at Owner's expense.

7. Trainer reserves right to notify Owner within seven (7) days of arrival if horse, in Trainer's opinion, is deemed dangerous, handicapped, or untrainable; in such cause, Owner is responsible for removing horse within seven (7) days and all expenses incurred during horse's stay. After all fees have been paid in full, Contract is concluded.

8. Horse Shows: Trainer is not authorized to show horse, Trainer will have horse shown at his sole discretion, Trainer will show horse at mutually agreed upon shows. Trainer shall provide transportation at $_____ per mile, plus $_____ per show, minimum charge per show $_____ . Professional horse transportation fees, if, used, will be paid by Owner.

9. Owner shall pay horse's entry fees, ground fees, stall fees, an "overnite" fee consisting of $_____ per night and/or an allocation representing the ratio of Owner's horse to total horses being a shown by Trainer multiplied by expenses incurred while staying overnite (ie: 1/12 x $700), and all other expenses incurred while being shown or transported.

10. Distribution of prize money shall be determined by custom of the show circuit.   Owner shall receive all trophies and ribbons. Trainer shall receive all prize money except futurities, maturities and versatilities where Owner shall first recover his entry fee from his horse's winnings and any excess shall be equally divided between Owner and Trainer.
☐ Other_____

11. It is agreed that should horse die, be sold by Owner or become unfit to train, trainer has the option of accepting another horse, according to paragraphs 6 and 7, as replacement within seven (7) days; or, making all fees due and payable whereas this Contract is concluded upon payment of fees in full.

12. Training and commencement of this Contract shall begin on or about_____ , and this Contract shall be concluded on or about and/or when _____ Owner and/or Trainer may terminate this Contract for any reason, after the minimum training period and with thirty (30) days written notice to the other. Trainer shall be paid for all fees incurred up to termination date. After all fees have been paid in full, Contract is concluded.

13. It is the Owner's responsibility to carry full insurance coverage on his horse and all personal property.

14. Should either party breach this contract, the breaching party shall pay for the other's court costs and attorney's fees related to such breach.

15. This Agreement is non-assignable and non-transferrable, except as stated above. This Contract is made and entered into the State of_____ and shall be enforced and interpreted under the laws of this state. Should any clause above be in conflict with State Law, that individual clause shall be null and void.

16. This Contract represents the entire agreement between the parties. No other agreements or promises, verbal or implied are included unless specifically stated in this written Contract. Additional agreements should be individually initialled by each party. If none, check box ☐ .

When Trainer and Owner and Owner's parent or guardian, if owner is a minor, sign this Contract, it will then be binding on both parties, subject to the above terms and conditions.

X_____
    Trainer (or authorized agent's) Signature

X_____
    Owner (or authorized agent's) Signature

X_____
    Owner's Parent or Guardian (if owner is a minor) Signature

_____
Owner's Address and Telephone

_____

_____

_____

_____
Description of Horse

Deposit of $_____ received on_____ by_____

Boarding Contract

This BOARDING CONTRACT is made and entered into on this_____ day of _____, 199_____, by and between_____, hereinafter designated "Manager," and_____, hereinafter designated "Owner," and if Owner is a minor, Owner's parent or guardian_____. Manager agrees to accept Owner's horse_____, Reg. No._____ for boarding; and, it is the plan and intention Owner to board this horse. For and in consideration of the agreements hereinafter set forth, Owner and Manager mutually agree as follows:

1. Owner agrees that Manager_____ (Farm) their agents and employees are not liable for death, sickness and/or accident, including consequential damages, caused to horse, except if caused by the willful and wanton gross negligence of Manager. In addition, Owner agrees to hold Manager completely harmless and not liable for any injury whatsoever caused to Owner, and/or any loss or damage to personal property.

2. It is the Owner's responsibility to carry full and complete insurance coverage on Owner, Owner's horse and all personal property. Owner agrees to abide by all manager's rules and regulations and wear proper safety equipment. (i.e, hard hat)

3. Owner shall pay Manager for boarding services, as described below, $_____ per month or $_____ per day. Marked boxes indicate services included in Board. Services NOT included in Board are priced to the left, and/or described below;

_____ ☐ Stall ☐ Large ☐ Small	_____	☐ Use of Facilities
_____ ☐ Bedding and cleaning	_____	☐ Vet/farrier handling
_____ ☐ Grain ☐ Hay	_____	☐ Turning out
_____ ☐ Regular feedings	_____	☐ Blanketing
_____ ☐ Clipping	_____	☐ Tack cleaning
_____ ☐ Show ☐ Body	_____	☐ Exercising
_____ ☐ Fans	_____	☐ Grooming
_____ ☐ Tacking up and cooling down	_____	☐ Lessons
	_____	☐ Private
_____ ☐ Wormings	_____	☐ Group
_____ ☐ Use of pasture	_____	☐ Semi-private

4. Board is due on the first (1st) proceeding month, timely payments are strictly enforced. A late fee of $_____ Will be charged on payments received more than seven (7) days late; plus a finance charge of 1½% per month (18% annually) will be charged on all accounts 30 days past due. If payment is overdue by 90 days, Manager is entitled to a lien against horse for amount due and shall enforce lien and sell horse for amount due, according to the appropriate laws of the state. A security deposit of $_____ , payable with this contract, shall be refunded to Owner within thirty (30) days of completion of contract.

5. Horse shall be free from infectious, contagious or transmissible disease. Required: current negative Coggins Test, Veterinarian's health certificate, a health, worming and immunization record. Manager reserves the right to refuse horse if not in proper health.

6. Manager reserves the right to notify the Owner within seven (7) days of horse's arrival if horse, in Manager's opinion, is deemed dangerous, sick or undesirable for a boarding stable. In such case, Owner is responsible for removing horse within seven (7) days and for all fees incurred during horse's stay. After all fees have been paid, this Contract is concluded.

7. Regular veterinarian and farrier attention will be arranged by Manager, Owner, and shall be invoiced by Manager, Veterinarian and Farrier directly to Owner. In the event of sickness and/or accident to the horse, after reasonable efforts have failed to contact Owner, Manager has permission to contact a veterinarian for treatment.

8. If horse dies, is sold, or upon thirty (30) days written notice to Manager after this date _____, Owner may terminate this Contract for any reason. In such case, Manager shall be paid all fees incurred up to termination date. After all fees have been paid in full, this Contract is concluded. If proper notice is not given, manager shall keep security deposit and consider it liquidated damage.

9. Commencement of this Contract shall begin on or about _____, and be concluded on or about _____ and/or when Manager or Owner give thirty (30) days written notice to conclude the contract.

10. This Contract is non-assignable and non-transferable. If stable shuts down, Manager will give Owner thirty (30) days written notice and Manager will be held harmless.

11. Should either party breach this contract, the breaching party shall pay for the others court costs and attorney's fees related to such breach.

12. This Contract is made and entered into the State of _____ and shall be enforced and interpreted under the laws of this state. Should any clause be in conflict with State Law, that individual clause is null and void.

13. This Contract represents the entire agreement between the parties. No other agreements or promises, verbal or implied, are included unless specifically stated in this written agreement. Additional agreements should be separately initialled by each party. If none, chech box .

When Manager and Owner and Owner's parent or guardian, if Owner is a minor, sign this Contract, it will then be binding on both parties, subject to the above terms and conditions.

_____
Manager's (or authorized agent's) Signature

Owner's (or authorized agent's) Signature

_____
Address & Telephone of Owner

Owner's Parent/Guardian if owner is a minor

Security deposit of $_____ received on _____ by _____

CERTIFICATE OF REGISTRATION

THE AMERICAN QUARTER HORSE ASSOCIATION
Amarillo, Texas 79168

NAME	REGISTRATION NUMBER	STATE FOALED
STORYS BEAU DIDLEY	2476780	MARYLAND

COLOR	SEX	FOALED
SORREL	GELDING	JANUARY 22, 1986

BREEDER	AQHA ID NUMBER	CITY	STATE
BINETTE CAROL F	0525950	LA PLATA	MARYLAND

OWNER	AQHA ID NUMBER	CITY	STATE
BINETTE CAROL F	0525950	LA PLATA	MARYLAND

STORY MAN
- GO MAN GO 82000
  - 616226
- SPANISH TALE 197000

SIRE
STORYS REFLECTION 1196060

MISS REVIVE
- ARRIVE TP
  - 97465
- MISS REVENUE 58103

BEATLE BOY HANK
- BEATLE LUCK 306360
  - 1086549
- IAN MARIA HANK 746894

DAM
BEATLES BAR FRIDAY 1350519

VAN'S MAGGIE BARS
- STAR VAN 93902
  - 907541
- BARS SISSY 346923

MARKINGS
STAR AND STRIP. SNIP. LEFT FORE SOCK LEFT HIND PASTERN WHITE. NO OTHER MARKINGS.

This is to certify that the above named and described horse has been registered in the Stud Book of The American Quarter Horse Association. This certificate is issued in reliance on a written application submitted and attested by the owner at time of foaling: and upon the express condition that the Association has the privilege to correct and/or cancel this certificate for cause under its rules and regulations.

DATE ISSUED
OCTOBER 28, 1986   EXECUTIVE VICE-PRESIDENT

TRANSFER RECORD
The last name entered hereunder is the present owner of this horse as shown on the records of The American Quarter Horse Association. To transfer the within described horse, make transfer on a separate transfer form or bill of sale, which will be furnished free by the ASSOCIATION. Send it to the office of the American Quarter Horse Association ------ along with the registration certificate and the transfer fee, The transfer of ownership will then he made on this certificate and mailed as instructed.

FOR OFFICE USE ONLY — DO NOT WRITE ON THIS CERTIFICATE

Date of Purchase	Name and Address of Owner as Shown by Transfer Record	Attest of Record by Secretary
2, 476,780 07/09/95	POST JOHN D ID# 0112233 AVELLA, PENNSYLVANIA	
2, 476,780 07/09/95	CABALLE ANDREA ID# 2145598 PITTSBURGH, PENNSYLVANIA	

CERTIFICATE OF REGISTRATION CON'T.

MARKINGS OF HORSE
WHICH THIS REGISTRATION
CERTIFICATE HAS BEEN ISSUED

DO NOT ALTER MARKINGS
ON THIS CERTIFICATE

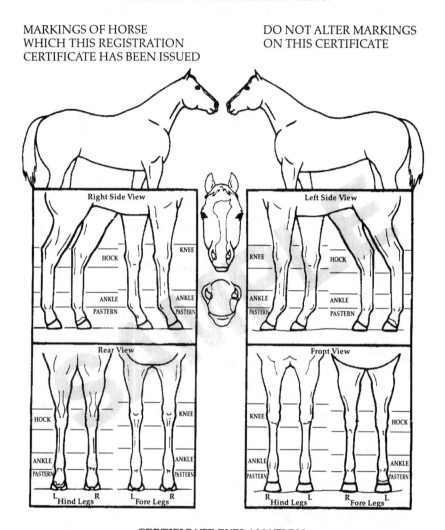

CERTIFICATE EXPLANATION

THIS CERTIFICATE OF REGISTRATION IS ISSUED UNDER ASSOCIATION REGULATIONS WHICH ARE FULLY EXPLAINED IN THE OFFICIAL HANDBOOK.

ANY HORSE RECEIVING A REGISTRATION NUMBER AND RECEIVING THIS CERIFICATE SHALL BE ELIGIBLE FOR BREEDING AND PERFORMING IN RECONGNIZED EVENTS.

AMERICAN QUATER HORSE ASSOCIATION
AMARILLO, TEXAS 79169

CATAHOOCHEE

1990 16.1 Hand Appendix Gelding

NOW OFFERED FOR SALE

YOU SHOULD PLACE A
PHOTO OF
HORSE AND RIDER
HERE

PLACE A
CLOSEUP
PHOTO OF
HORSE HERE

WENDY LEESER and
ROBIN WEATHERBY

Amateur

- Hunter Under Saddle
- Hunt Seat Equitation
- Showmanship
- Senior Hunter Under Saddle

Looking For A Hunt Seat Horse with the Competitive Edge?

Watch for Robin, Wendy and Real Jammies at the 1996 Two Year Old Hunt Seat Futurities

Contact: Robin Weatherby
717-274-5508 Evenings, Lebanon, PA

THREE OAKS QUARTER HORSES
Tracey Baker, Elizabethtown, PA